FEDERALISM AND FEDERATION

Federalism and Federation

PRESTON KING

THE JOHNS HOPKINS UNIVERSITY PRESS
BALTIMORE, MARYLAND

First published in the United States of America, 1982,
by The Johns Hopkins University Press,
Baltimore, Maryland 21218

First published in Great Britain, 1982,
by Croom Helm Ltd, 2-10 St John's Road, London SW11

Library of Congress Catalog Card Number 82-47974
ISBN 0-8018-2922-4
    0-8018-2923-2 (pbk)

Printed and bound in Great Britain

CONTENTS

1. Introduction   9

Part One: Federalism as Ideology   17
2. Federalist Pluralism   19
3. Centralist Federalism   24
4. Decentralist Federalism   39
5. Federalist Balance   56

Part Two: Federation as Institution   69
6. Analysis, Norms and Facts   71
7. Democracy Qualified   88
8. Contracting Out   96
9. Secession Nullified   108
10. Centralization by Degree   121

Part Three: Conclusion   131
11. Classifying Federations   133
12. Postscript   146

Bibliography   149

Index   156

To Chevene and Carol
and
In Memory
of
Allen

1 INTRODUCTION

The study of politics is conventionally divided into political philosophy and political science, where the first of these is said to concern values and the second, facts. A similar distinction is that established between political philosophy and political theory, where the first is held to be normative and the second empirical. The resuscitation of political philosophy as a normative enterprise is often regarded as coextensive with the injection anew of moral commitment into the rump of political study. Stout support for political science as an empirical endeavour is often regarded as similar to the objective knowledge of medicines and their properties without which rumps and the rest, in taking ill, would more speedily expire. There is of course much to be said for moral commitment and no less for factual knowledge.

One problem arises, however, where normative and empirical commitments are imagined to be flatly and mutually incompatible. Though they betray distinct emphases, it is as well to note that they cannot be mutually exclusive. Political, economic and social behaviour is all to do with human action, and human action, in the way in which it usually and distinctively interests us, is purposive. Behaviour such as this always reflects some moral concern. At the same time, human behaviour does not start from scratch with the dawn of each new day: there are regularities to be observed, descriptive generalizations made − even modest 'predictions' or 'forecasts' may respectably be ventured.

To say that we ought to perform an act presupposes that we can. If the 'ought' is taken to be normative, and the 'can' to be empirical, it will be obvious that we cannot intelligibly issue normative pronouncements where we have no grasp of their related empirical underpinnings. On the other hand, if we seek only to describe the 'facts' − whether in the singular or in general or universally − it is essential to recognize that facts are infinite, that none is self-evident, and that all are and can only be perceived within and in contrast to established perceptive categories. (We cannot meaningfully discuss the 'fact' of Everest without some prior convention about the meaning of 'mountain', nor the victory of President Reagan without some prior convention about the meaning of 'election'.) Categories of perception, however, are selective. They include, but also exclude. To apply them is to choose. Any act of choice may be subject to the pronouncement that it ought or ought not to be exercised. No newspaper prints *all* the facts. It prints *some* of the facts. It does not even have access to 'all the facts'. It has access only to some but must still choose which of these its editors regard as 'fit to print'. The pursuit of any discovery, or pronouncement of any 'fact', in as far as it is necessarily subject to choice, cannot escape moral involvement merely by virtue of being 'factual'. It is not logically possible, therefore, to engage in normative or empirical pursuits in such a manner that the one may entirely exclude the other.

An acceptable distinction may be made between normative and empirical theory, then, in as far as the emphasis of the one is upon rightness of action and the other upon validity of fact. It none the less remains that each of these two categories of judgement presupposes the other. Besides normative and empirical emphasis, however, account must also be taken of logic, of an 'analytical' theory or emphasis. Analytical Theory is not an area of concern to which students of politics and society have been disposed to direct undue attention. This is not to say they have been able to operate without actually resorting to it. It is only to say that this utilization has not been resorted to in any strikingly self-conscious manner. There is reason in this for urging more generally the merits of Analytical Theory. The present essay does not do this. It does, however, illustrate the manner in which an analytical emphasis might operate in an important politico-legal subject area — the area namely of federal union.

Analytical political theory differs from normative and empirical theory in the same way that these differ from one another: by emphasis. Just as any normative pronouncement presupposes empirical possibility, so it presupposes logical coherence. Just as any empirical pursuit presupposes alternative pursuits, and the morality of choice implicit in any such commitment, so does empirical discourse presuppose logical coherence. Value, fact, and logic: the three are intertwined. And the emphasis of Analytical Theory is upon logic.

One of our concerns in any statement that pretends to objectivity is to avoid inconsistency or self-contradiction. It is as useless saying that 'the Iranian government will fall *and* not fall tomorrow', as saying that 'the Iranian government will fall *or* not fall tomorrow'. Neither formula tells us anything. Many students of social science, envious of the success of physics and other natural sciences, think that all they really need do is move in the direction of increasing quantification — and empiricism so understood. This disposition has declined over the past decade and more, but it is still kicking and it is understandable that it should. It is useless saying anything about the speed of light or about the value of gold per ounce or about the volume of a meteor, if we cannot count or weigh or measure. Measurement in so many respects is still — obviously and trivially — crucial. The trouble is that in insisting upon measurement we may, in certain disciplines, get ahead of ourselves. It may prove useful in particular to pull the social sciences up short — and ask: *what* are we measuring?

It is probable that in most branches of the social sciences we have taken quantification rather further than we have taken logical analysis. It is all very well, for example, to compare federations, and to apply large-scale hypotheses in the process, such as that they are only formed and maintained when the social forces opposing and supporting unity are roughly equal; or that they only emerge where there is some domestic or external military threat to the territorial units from which the federation is formed. The trouble is that the identity of a federation has not the obviousness of a stone, a tree, a sand-dune or any other physical object. Attempts to measure the behaviour of federations (as of any other forms of social organization) must inevitably involve some tacit or explicit conventions or agreements about what a federation actually is. But the most characteristic phenomenon in federal studies today is for observers to ignore or to deny the possibility of conventions (definition) while pushing on beyond this to attempt to say much of substance about — indeed to measure — the phenomenon.

Many observers are opposed to logical exposition on the assumption that it merely derives from personal bias. If this is so, then the same objection may be levelled against descriptive accounts — that they too derive from personal bias. After all, the data to be described are legion; the range of factual propositions is infinite; we can place no numbered limit upon them. Description accordingly cannot be transparently automatic; it is selective. Selection can only be engaged in from some perspective, which brings us back to personal bias. The object of the exercise is not at all to maintain that all description is vanity, but only that one cannot regard its status as either superior to or independent of logical analysis. Description always implies analysis. And to the extent that the analysis is incoherent, so shall the description prove disjointed. To describe is to place observations in categories, or to categorize observations: no matter the precedence. The object of analysis must be to axiomatize categories — principally so that they do not overlap. No empirical understanding of society can proceed without conventions: convention is the price we pay for such understanding. No description of reality can proceed beyond the bounds of language: the concept of 'reality' is itself linguistic. It is useless to imagine that all we need do to understand federation is to somersault into some description of the behaviour of federations. How can we say what this behaviour is without some coherent and relevant convention regarding the subject whose behaviour we commit ourselves to describing? The supposed empiricist who cannot bother himself with such niceties finds himself in the end out on a limb — often displaying a flurry of impressive activity which cannot lead to any coherent conclusion. Why, for example, enquire whether federations empirically promote liberty where one unreflectingly assumes that they are necessarily and comprehensively democratic? Why enquire whether federations are unstable if we unreflectingly assume them to be fully sovereign? Why should we assume federations to arise only in response to threat if we unreflectingly regard them all as freely contractual? Can we coherently maintain that the basic cause of the rise and survival of federations is an *a priori* commitment to union *per se* while simultaneously suggesting that the chief reason is the prospect of military, diplomatic and economic expansion shared by contractants?

We may take it that 'science' is nothing more than 'scientia' — knowledge or knowing. We may take it too, however, that different types of knowledge are appropriate to the different subjects to which they may relate. A knowledge of inanimate objects cannot quite prove the same as knowledge of sentient and self-conscious beings like humans. We may have knowledge of both physics and politics. In neither case can we assume that the 'facts' disgorged in these fields are self-evident. It is only by reference to conventions that we can know what a 'fact' is. Gin and vodka look alike but do not taste the same. The waters of London and Nairobi also look alike but do not taste the same. It is no more 'self-evident' that gin and vodka are different than that 'water' in Nairobi and London is identical. The first two are different, the second two identical, by virtue of conventions relating to the meaning of 'gin', 'vodka' and 'water'. A similar situation obtains with respect to notions like 'filth', 'weeds', 'helpfulness' and so on. We cannot use these expressions without tacit or explicit conventions governing the manner in which we do so. All knowledge, and science taken as such, depends upon conventions.

Note the difference however between a science of inanimate objects, on the one hand, and a science of self-conscious human subjects, on the other. To make factual assertions about either requires conventions. It is only by having a coherent and exclusive, but not necessarily explicit, notion of what we mean by 'water' that we can proceed to test its characteristic behaviour in other respects — as by noting the temperature at which it boils or that at which it freezes. If we seek to determine the rate of speed at which stones fall when dropped from the garage roof, we shall of course require some convention relating to the nature of a 'stone', minimally to avoid the confusion which would attend confounding stones with, perhaps, small grey balloons filled with helium. On the whole, however, establishing conventions of this sort does not represent so great a problem.

Suppose, by contrast, we take notions like 'tribe', 'nation', 'state', 'government', 'sovereignty', 'independence', 'pressure group', 'faction', 'party', 'democracy', 'federalism' and so on. In all such cases we encounter far greater difficulty. First, and most obviously, we do not normally take such items to be physical objects. We may speak happily enough of parties being formed or of governments falling, but it remains that no one has ever heard or seen or felt or tasted or caught the scent — of these parties in formation or governments in collapse. *Mr* Reagan on the morning of 20 January 1981 was not *observed* to look different from *President* Reagan in the afternoon of the same day. Yet, the change of title signalled a change of government. Something no doubt was observed, but something qualitatively different from water on the boil or a stone cleaving the air.

In as far as parties and governments are observable, it is only by reference to certain criteria which establish what is to count as a party or a government. Beyond this, such observation presupposes as subjects conscious agents who are themselves directed by principles of right or correct action. Thus, when we advance criteria regarding what is to count as a party or government — or indeed a federation — we must do so initially in the light of those principles by which the subjects involved conceive themselves to be guided. It will be clear that subjects profess beliefs to which they may or may not adhere, as also that they often act in a manner consistent with principles which they simply omit to profess or, more strongly, profess to reject. The fact is (1) that social institutions are constituted of clusters of principles which are never given an absolute priority ranking *vis-à-vis* one another and (2) that these principles, even where accorded a priority ranking, must be constantly applied to new cases where the outcome of such application cannot, in the nature of things, be altogether predictable. The upshot is that acceptable conventions distinguishing specific social 'facts' are far more difficult — but no less necessary — to establish than conventions regarding physical 'things'. The conclusion we draw is that the observer of social phenomena must not only impose criteria in order to observe phenomena, but must do so in a manner which takes due account of the fact that the phenomena observed are not inert but sentient, conscious and self-legislating.

If we seek to determine the characteristic behaviour of federations in formation or subsequently, we require as indicated a defensible convention relating to the nature of a 'federation'. Otherwise, what we discover may be vitiated by confusing federations with other types of state. In establishing such a convention, however, it is essential that we take due account of those beliefs or principles current within or about federations regarding the character of these institutions. To do this raises genuine difficulties which at points appear insuperable, although they are not quite so in fact. Nothing demonstrates the difficulties more clearly than a survey of the literature on federal theory and practice. While stones have a way of lying quite still, holding themselves out to inspection, federations, like all human institutions, are not so obliging. Federations move, they change, and this movement is equally reflected in the views of those who operate and study them, as where federations over time are variably stipulated to be 'contractual', 'democratic', 'dual', 'co-operative', 'new', 'centralized', 'peripheralized' and so on.

Let those worry about 'essentialism' who will. The dangers of circularity, regression and hair-splitting in any logical analysis are of course as real as having an accident in fast-moving traffic. One who lives a long way from work has to take the risk. One who seeks to achieve empirical understanding in the social sciences must climb aboard an analytical vehicle to satisfy the first condition for getting home. If we were to regard all federations as fundamentally dissimilar, we could not compare them; if we are to compare them, we must establish for them a defensible common identity. To locate such an identity we must not only impose criteria, but must pick our way through the various principles held within and about federations. We need not maintain that all human behaviour is rule-governed to maintain that federations and the like cannot be understood in any other terms.

The rules governing federations cannot be exactly those professed by actors and proponents, since these rules are not altogether consistent, nor ranked in a wholly firm order of priority. But neither can the observer's criteria be totally at odds with those professed by actors and proponents within federations, since this would imply that federal institutions involve no element of conscious self-direction. It is in this regard that the acceptance of the constitutional character of federations must prove so important, a constitutionality both written and unwritten, explicit and tacit. Any attempt to overleap the question of constitutional identity must involve ignoring the element of conscious self-direction characteristic of federal and all other human institutions. In short, any attempt empirically to study the political behaviour of federal 'societies', by way of omitting some prior location of the institutional and indeed constitutional identity which renders these societies 'federal', involves a fundamental misconception.

It only remains to say that this book is genuinely introductory, in that it actually begins at the beginning. Such a beginning, however, is not to be construed as non-argumentative. On the contrary, the most fundamental, important and contentious of arguments will be located precisely here, rather than at some more distant point along the path of federal research. There has accumulated a vast literature on the subject of federal theory and practice, a good proportion of it insightful and acute in various ways. An introduction of this kind could not be written without recourse to such an array of prior analysis and observation. Omission of the usual acknowledgements may be excused: the selectiveness enjoined must prove invidious against a backdrop of numerous, undeserved omissions, on levels both personal and professional. Some omission of the usual signs of respect to opposed positions is equally to be excused: that a position is countered at all must be taken to imply in virtually every case that it is not a 'man of straw' and thus deserves attention.

PART ONE

FEDERALISM AS IDEOLOGY

The way is like an empty vessel
That yet may be drawn from.

(Lao Tzu)

2 FEDERALIST PLURALISM

There are many varieties of pluralism of which federalism may be taken to constitute one sub-set. We have no space here to treat pluralism as such in great detail. In any event, a fuller discussion of pluralism has been provided elsewhere. Suffice it to say that the basic varieties of pluralism are:

(1) the doctrine of separation of powers;
(2) the doctrine of checks and balances;
(3) the argument for plural party systems;
(4) the ideology of corporatism;
(5) the device of proportional representation;
(6) the doctrine of social pluralism (which encompasses the idea of crosscutting cleavages or of multiple affiliations); and
(7) the doctrine of federalism.

Our present concern is, of course, principally with this last notion, and only with the others where the treatment of our subject appears to require it.*

There are several variations on federalism but each of these tends to be marked by a concern with territorial representation and, most especially, the representation of regional units in the national legislature. What we shall be concerned to do in this chapter is to explore the range of federal ideologies — basically centralism, decentralism and balance — which will be discussed separately and in greater detail below (in chapters 3, 4 and 5 respectively). It is only following this review that we shall advance to inspect more directly the phenomenon of federal union in Part Two.

An ideology is a broad and reasonably coherent set of ideas which is invoked with a view to mobilizing and directing political action in order to serve some relatively specific purpose. Ideology may be imagined as a broad outlook to which specific and practical socio-political applications are attached. There can scarcely be any practical activity or commit-

---

*These varieties of pluralism are dealt with more fully in a separate book on *Pluralism* in this series.

ment which does not reflect a broader outlook nor indeed any genuinely broad outlook which does not somehow reveal itself in practical activity. The implication of this is that any mobilizational call at all for war or peace, to defend good or evil, whether for now or forever − is almost certainly *pro tanto* ideological. Most of us, if only occasionally, employ 'ideology' in this large (and weak) sense, and not Martin Seliger (1976) only. Some of us, however, even if simultaneously, are disposed to employ the expression in a narrow (and strong) sense, where we intend in particular an *a priori* or universalist style of argument which, while being logically immune to criticism, seeks to secure in practice either social change or stasis (cp. King 1968). In as far as federalism is concerned to recommend anything at all, it is clear that it is ideological, at least in a weak sense. But, beyond this, a case can easily be made to show that much of the argument to do with federalism is ideological in the strong sense, too.

In the present discussion, 'federalism' is distinguished from 'federation'. Such a distinction has been advanced before, if in marginally different ways. A. Marc (1961) argues that federalism 'became a doctrine' in the nineteenth century (p. 14) and salutes Proudhon as the first of these doctrinaires. He does not actually wish for federalism to be understood as an 'idéologie' − that is to say, following his conception of the matter, as totalistic, *a priori*, closed and unpragmatic. But he does seek to promote federalism as a comprehensive philosophy of 'diversity in unity' (p. 64) in order to provide 'this revolutionary awareness which is today the *sine qua non* of our salvation' (p. 117). Marc presumably implies in all this a distinction between federalist philosophy and concrete sets of federal institutions. Bernard Voyenne (1976) is more specific in arguing that 'the federalist idea, as Proudhon was to show, is organised anarchy' and that 'the history of this idea is not, by a long chalk, that of federations' (pp. 21–2). The fact, however, that a few writers have been inclined to make this distinction between federalism and federation is in no way to suggest that most do − for most make no distinction at all.

The important consideration is merely that 'federalism' is often promoted as a political philosophy of diversity-in-unity, while being equally often merely observed and described as an institutional matter of fact with no particular concern for either promoting or undermining such a form of unity. Very often, too, it will be both recommended and observed simultaneously. Where we recognize these differences of emphasis, it should not be difficult to concede the utility of differential labelling. Accordingly, 'federalism' is employed where the interest is primarily ideological (whether in the weak or strong sense), while 'federation' is applied to designate a more descriptive, institutional arrangement of fact, without particular regard to whether it is being supported or opposed. Much of the argument 'Against Federalism' is most relevantly directed against the strong ideological assumption that federalism is always or usually the best or most appropriate of conceivable institutional arrangements (cp. Laski 1939; Jackson 1941; Riker 1964: esp. 155).

There are several writers today who will advise us that 'federalism is not an intellectual doctrine' (R. Aron and H. Brugmans, in Brugmans 1969) or that 'federalism is not an ideology' (Deuerlein 1972: 332). This sort of protest normally need not detain us, as long as we substitute federation for federalism. Sometimes, however, the claim that federalism is non-ideological is intended to convey that federalism is weakly ideological in the sense of being pragmatic or supportive of compromise. The problem here is that pragmatism and compromise *may* be taken as universal principles, and where that happens, they become automatically closed *a priori*, and thus ideological in the strong sense. Where it is only meant that pragmatism and compromise are generally appropriate, this can still be construed as representing a weak sense of what is commonly meant by 'ideological'. Federalism becomes all the more obviously and strongly ideological where an exponent assumes democracy to be the only just form of political organization and where it is contended that 'federalism is the necessary consequence of democracy' (Brugmans 1969: 39).

Ideological *federalism* (as distinct from institutional *federation*) reflects at least three different mobilizational orientations – the first being *centralist*, the second *decentralist*, while the third involves an appeal to *balance*. Federalism, most distinctively, constitutes a variable response to opposed demands for the dispersal and concentration of power. More precisely, federalism constitutes a variable response to opposed demands for the centralization and decentralization of power on a specifically territorial basis.

An ideology of *centralism* can be advanced universally, and is most aptly referred to as the doctrine of 'absolutism', perhaps of 'totalitarianism'. A specifically federalist ideology of centralism can only *appear* to be advanced universally (as by Lionel Curtis and R.M. Hutchins) – for the intended reach (or degree) of such centralism is not 'absolute', nor is it 'total'. The apparently universally centralist federalism of writers like Hutchins and Curtis may contain an important *a priori* element. It is the case that a major assumption underlying their outlook is that independent power centres, possessed of their own instruments of war, always represent a threat to one another and therefore to peace. It is this assumption which leads to the conclusion that the best means of overcoming the threat consists in eliminating the potential which 'independent' national states necessarily possess for engaging in war. The doctrine of sovereignty, however, as expounded by figures like Bodin and Hobbes, maintains at points that no integration which is incomplete can be stable — that is, it urges that all power be transferred to the centre. By contrast, the argument of *apparently* universal centralizing federalists — those who seek world government — is that the most stable (and solely feasible) form of integration is that which is partial — and which does not attempt to be absolute or total. In short, even where federalist centralism is demanded universally (as for world government), it never represents a call for complete and unrestricted centralization. The most that federalist proponents of world government can be reproached with is the universal recommendation of some form of 'balance' — as between demands for a global governmental centre and the retention of certain degrees of peripheral national autonomy. The federalist appeal for world government is effectively for some form of partial, never total, centralization. For this reason, even the most extreme appeals for *federalist centralism* must remain ideologically weak, if we choose to label them ideological at all. (A universal appeal for balance is not the same of course as a universal appeal for unending integration, and is a position that requires to be inspected independently.)

Most federalist centralism is not even of an apparently universal kind. It evokes recommendations which are restricted in time and space. Such is the case with that famous American document, *The Federalist*. In as far as this work's support of centralism is ideological, it is only weakly so. Its contention is not that the only possible type of stable polity is federal. The authors, in fact (as Davis 1978 points out), were not even clear about the distinctiveness of the new institutions they were fashioning. They were only concerned to maintain that the new American constitution, whether labelled 'federal' or otherwise, provided a solution to the problem of unity in circumstances where the complete integration demanded by the more traditional doctrine of sovereignty was simply unattainable. This non-universal, and therefore weak, federalist form of centralism does provide, in a way, some kind of objection to the more sweeping tenets of universal, *a priori* centralism as represented by the classical sovereignty doctrine. But the implicit objection to *a priori* centralism contained in a work like *The Federalist* reflects less of a concern to overthrow the doctrine of sovereignty than to amend it — and

.indeed less even of a concern to amend it than to show how the new American arrangements were consistent with the traditional demands of the older doctrine. Taken as an amendment to the doctrine of sovereignty, of *a priori* and unlimited centralism, it will again be clear that the pragmatic federalist centralism of particular countries, in as far as it is ideological at all, is only weakly so. The original idea of a federal America or a federal Brazil or, today, of a federal Europe, was not and is not so much to divide and disperse, as to centralize and integrate — yet not in any abstract and unlimited degree.

An ideology of *decentralism* can be advanced universally. Just as the universal demand for unlimited centralism implies an 'absolutism', so the universal demand for a never-ceasing decentralism implies an 'anarchism'. While federalist centralism — whether promoted nationally or globally — is ideologically weak, the ideologies of absolutism and anarchism are of the strongest possible kind. Well-known proponents of universal federalist decentralism have often been known — and have most often called themselves — anarchists (e.g. Bakunin and Kropotkin), underlining the identity between such decentralism and anarchism. Just as all centralism is not universal and absolutist in its thrust (witness federalist centralism), neither is all decentralism ultimately anarchistic. What we may accept, however, is that any argument for a universal and *a priori* decentralism is as untenable as the parallel argument for a universal and *a priori* centralism: any two such arguments contradict and exclude one another. An ideological case of the strongest kind has never been made for centralist federalism. The case that has been and can be made for the universal appeal of decentralist and balanced federalism gives no promise of being tenable.

Decentralist and balanced federalisms are not very different in their implications, since the implied immobilism of any genuine balance (equilibrium) is also anarchical. If federalism is recommended to us as a philosophy of balance, the balance in question is of course between centralism and decentralism. Assuming such balance to imply an equality between them, then neither can prevail. Such an equilibrium in fact replicates the anarchist model of every individual or agent within a system enjoying a perfectly equal power with every other, such that none, not even a majority, can prevail. Where the recommendation for balance is not really for balance, where it is not intended that the sum of justice is mere equilibrium, then the most relevant label for this concern — one not easily dealt with in simple quantitative terms — is constitutionalism, understood as a key aspect of the larger subject of justice.

3 CENTRALIST FEDERALISM

Federalism may represent an argument for a certain type of centralization. This is the chief burden of *The Federalist* (1788). At the point of its publication, the independence or liberty of the original 13 American states already existed. The new item sought was 'a more enduring union'. The recommendations advanced by 'Publius' (the pseudonym of Alexander Hamilton, as assisted by James Madison and John Jay) all called for closer union, or greater centralization, than existed before. The arguments advanced for such increased centralization were several and various, but the most important were to the effect that closer union would secure a better defence against external threats, against war between the states, and against 'domestic faction and insurrection', while simultaneously providing a more solid base for external trade and private prosperity. 'Publius' expected that rival claims upon the Indian territories in the West would lead to war between the several states were they not brought under a central 'umpire or common judge to interpose between the contending parties' (no. 7). It does not much matter that 'Publius' was mistaken in relation to any assumption that union would entirely remove such a risk. The point is that the central argument was for a more centralized, efficient and powerful government.

The practical concern of *The Federalist* was not so much to defend as to restrict the individual liberty of the original 13 American states. There was the charge that the new American constitution 'would tend to render the government of the union too powerful', in reply to which *The Federalist* maintained that it was really the state authorities (by contrast with the national) which would tend to exercise the greatest hold upon the citizenry, and thus that 'it will always be far more easy for the state governments to encroach upon the national authorities, than for the national government to encroach upon the state authorities' (No. 17, Nos. 45 and 46). *The Federalist* argues – at least in the American context and perhaps generally – that the greater danger stems more from a powerful periphery than from a strong centre. 'A weak constitution must necessarily terminate in dissolution, for want of proper powers, or the usurpation of powers requisite for public safety' (No. 20). The contention here is that by making a central government too weak, one will likely force it to usurp the authority it requires to function as it ought, with this initial illegality preparing the ground for the unwanted evolution from republicanism to tyranny. There is nothing in any way anarchical about *The Federalist*. The great danger that it perceives is anarchy more than oppression, or better, the sort of oppression associated with anarchy. Indeed, 'the idea of governing at all times by simple force of law (which we have been told is the only admissible principle of republican government) has no place but in the reveries of those political doctors, whose sagacity disdains the admonitions of experimental instruction' (No. 28). The moral is Hobbesian, and it is firmly drawn. What was being advocated was less liberty than authority, less the desirability of states' rights than strong, responsible and centralized administration, less the danger to the states from the nation than the reverse.

The traditional doctrine of sovereignty argued for the illimitable concentration of power at a given centre, and that this power must be absolute, total, illimitable and indivisible. It is not for this sort of sovereignty that *The Federalist* argues. But it never attacks the doctrine of sovereignty *per se*. *The Federalist* declares itself 'in favor of an energetic government' (No. 23). Although the distinction between 'confederal' and 'federal' arrangements is not consistently or clearly maintained, the plain burden of the argument is to attack the tenability of confederal arrangements, to show that one cannot enjoy any form of stable government where such a government (whether called federal, central or national) is itself beholden to and dependent upon other sovereign states. Thus it holds 'a sovereign over sovereigns, a government over governments, a legislation for communities, as contradistinguished from individuals' to be absurd in theory and counterproductive in practice (No. 20). *The Federalist* basically argues against maintaining a central government based on a treaty arrangement between sovereign and independent states. It argues that such an arrangement puts the arbitrary interests of the states ahead of those of the citizenry as a whole, as also that the protection of the interests of the latter requires a central government possessed of the essential attributes of sovereignty.

The Federalist does not argue that for a government to be worthy of the name it must exercise total, absolute, illimitable and indivisible power in every sphere and degree. The argument is far more precise, in effect suggesting that a government need only hold sovereign sway in those areas of decision *assigned* to it — and that the areas assigned need not equate with *all* areas of decision. *The Federalist* does not expressly argue for the retention of individual state identities. It takes the survival of these for granted: 'the circumstances of our country are such, as to demand a compound instead of a simple . . . government'. It was understood that one simply could not erect, even were it desirable, a single system of government over an area so large and diverse as America. *The Federalist* was concerned to show, however, that one could construct a single and sovereign federal government out of a welter of state systems if one assumed that its function was partial and thus plainly stipulated what that function was to be by contrast with the powers to redound to the states: 'the essential point . . . will be to discriminate the objects . . . which shall appertain to the different provinces or departments of power' (No. 23). As to the 'objects' assigned to the national centre by *The Federalist*, they were merely less extensive than those assigned by Bodin and Hobbes — excluding for example any concern with control over religion and education. The chief objects assigned to the national centre by *The Federalist* were, basically, provision for common defence, a common foreign policy, and a common framework for internal and external trade. *The Federalist* argued that 'these powers' — the power to attend to these objects — 'ought to exist without limitation', that there should be 'no constitutional shackles' inhibiting their execution (No. 23). The union must have 'the power to exact obedience' from individuals and states (No. 21). There must be no limit on its powers of taxation in relation to the objects established. There must be no restrictions on legislative authority in providing for external defence (No. 26) nor 'in repelling those domestic dangers which may sometimes threaten the existence of state constitutions' (No. 21). In view of 'the endless diversities in the opinions of men' there must be a 'supreme tribunal' to which all conflicts between individuals and states can ultimately be referred. The important observation in all of this is not so much that *The Federalist* 'overthrew' the classical doctrine of sovereignty as that it attempted to demonstrate how far a union of American states would require to travel in order to become minimally 'sovereign'. Thus, although *The Federalist* accepts some notion of 'divided sovereignty', it does so on grounds of practical necessity, not as an ideal; and where it accepts such a notion, it is on the assumption that the centre can and must be fully sovereign in its sphere, which is to say in relation to those objects which define its function as a centre.

If it is the case that the object of *The Federalist* was more to accommodate than to overthrow the doctrine of sovereignty, the question arises as to how it could so commonly have been read as a document supportive of liberty. The answer must be that support for sovereignty and liberty are not necessarily to be seen as inconsistent. On the view of *The Federalist*, two items are necessary for a government: an end, and a means of achieving it. Take defence, external and internal, as the chief end. The power to tax must be the chief means towards securing this. As one cannot place limits on the potential danger, so one cannot place restrictions on the power to tax as the principal means of averting the danger. Hence a difficulty. If the federal power to tax is unrestricted, then it may acquire over time a monopoly, abolishing state taxes as an interference with its own, and so ending with 'the destruction of the state governments'. How did *The Federalist* answer? By suggesting, in effect, that it was not the liberty of the *states* which was to be protected, and that *their* liberty was not necessarily consistent with that of their citizens. More directly, the argument was that the state governments had greater power than the federal government; that the states were in no way formally restricted in their power to tax, and 'are invested with complete sovereignty'; that if the lack of such a restriction is a danger to liberty, then the state governments already posed such a threat; that if they did not pose such a threat, then the prospect that a federal government with like powers could do so was all the more improbable. How then did *The Federalist* conceive of liberty? The authors reflect a joint concern with the avoidance of tyranny and with securing self-government, both of which equate with a republican state of affairs. In effect, for *The Federalist*, freedom consisted in the electoral control of rulers by the ruled, that is in 'a due dependence of those who are to administer . . . upon the people'. Thus the chief guarantee of freedom, *The Federalist* argued, lay not in restricting the power or sovereignty of the government, but in securing that ultimate control of the government rest with the people. Thus, 'all observations founded upon the danger of usurpation, ought to be referred to the composition and structure of the government, not to the nature or extent of its powers' (No. 21).

The authors of *The Federalist* do not appear to have made any less of the doctrine of sovereignty than did their antecedents, nor to have made much more of the distinction between monarchy, aristocracy and democracy than did Hobbes. The basic assumption appears to have been that the attributes of sovereignty are the same in all cases. Obviously it was assumed that these diverse types of government are distinct, but also that the general attributes of sovereignty remain common to them all. Thus, if the monarch as sovereign has absolute, total, indivisible and illimitable power, then so have a sovereign people. For *The Federalist*, the guarantee of liberty basically consisted in the existence of republican government — in 'the due dependence' of rulers upon the ruled. 'The federal and state governments are in fact but different agents and trustees of the people, instituted with different powers, and designated for different purposes'. The federal and state governments were not 'mutual rivals and enemies . . . uncontrolled by any common superior'. The ultimate authority 'resides in the people alone' and decisions about whether the state or federal governments will enjoy the greater power must rest with them (No. 46). The preference that runs through *The Federalist* is for common national citizenship, not for separate sovereignties with their attendant confederal arrangements; for the entire citizenry as sovereign, together with a central (but not a single) government responsive to their sovereign demands. Quite simply, 'the fabric of American empire ought to rest on the solid basis of *the consent of the people*' (No. 22).

Although the authors of *The Federalist* were not concerned to promote centralization of an unqualified and illimitable kind, they were none the less implicitly sympathetic to the more important arguments advanced by earlier writers on sovereignty. The best summary statement from *The Federalist* on this matter reads as follows:

> A government ought to contain in itself every power requisite to the full accomplishment of the objects committed to its care, and to the complete execution of the trusts for which it is responsible; free from every other control, but a regard to the public good and to the sense of the people.
>
> As the duties of superintending the national defence and of securing the public peace against foreign or domestic violence, involve a provision for casualties and dangers, to which no possible limits can be assigned, the power of making that provision ought to know no other bounds than the exigencies of the nation and the resources of the community [No. 31].

The most important concern of *The Federalist*, then, was to promote efficient, centralized government, not to retain local, state identities; and to promote such government on the basis of popular consent, not via such delegated authority as might be grudgingly conceded by the states. Only secondarily, albeit still importantly, does *The Federalist* argue for defence against the national centre. The defence argued for is of four kinds, in descending order of significance: first, defence against centralist tyranny by deriving power from the people as a whole (not so much from the states); secondly, by dividing and balancing the power of the centre itself; third, by territorially dividing popularly sanctioned government between a national centre and various state localities; fourth, by dividing up the interests of various sections of the population so that no one of these can automatically (and thus unjustly) prevail. 'You must first enable the government to control the governed; and in the next place, oblige it to control itself. A dependence on the people is no doubt the primary control on the government; but experience has taught man the necessity of auxiliary precautions' (No. 51).

Basically, the argument of *The Federalist* is a centralist argument. It is in no way so dramatically centralist as the earlier arguments advanced by figures like Bodin, Hobbes, Grotius, Spinoza and Pufendorf in support of the doctrine of sovereignty. For *The Federalist* is in some degree concerned to defend against the dangers of centralism. But *The Federalist* in no way approaches the extremes of federalist anarchism aspired to by figures like Bakunin and Kropotkin. It does accord some importance to decentralism, *faute de mieux*, perhaps as a necessary evil, but not particularly in the form of an ideal to be achieved. The chief defence against centralist excess is perceived by *The Federalist* to consist in the way in which the centre itself is structured – in the division and balance of the component parts of the central power or government. We might say that this was less to do with the decentralization of power, conceived territorially, than with the division of power, located centrally, and this interest in the division (and balance) of power is in no way a distinctively federal concern, being perfectly applicable to non-federal arrangements.

The authors of *The Federalist* were concerned to promote centralism, and in effect used many of the traditional arguments embedded in the doctrine of sovereignty to drive their points home. At the same time, they were sufficiently aware of the dangers attending any concentration of power to want simultaneously to defend against these, and hence placed great emphasis both upon popular sovereignty and upon devising constitutional checks to inhibit such sovereignty. This dual orientation reflects a degree of incoherence. What is the source of this incoherence? It probably derives from the traditional formulation of the doctrine of sovereignty. Suppose that the only sort of government worth its salt is agreed to be 'sovereign', and that the chief features of a sovereign government are thought to consist in its possession of an absolute, total, illimitable and indivisible power. Suppose further that there are many different types of sovereign government – including democratic government (which can equally well be styled 'popular' or 'republican'). The implication would be that, where and if democratic government achieves sovereignty – that is endures over time on some stable basis – it must be as 'absolute' as any other form of government, such as monarchy. And this would suggest that there was as great a danger to individual liberty or freedom from a stable, that is sovereign, democratic regime as from a sovereign monarchy. If that were so, then of course one would require to have more than popular control to enjoy a genuine freedom. Hence the tergiversation as between 'a dependence on the people' as 'the primary control on the government' and the intelligence vouchsafed by experience relating to 'the need of auxiliary precautions'. This apparent paradox about stable 'democracies' being absolutely sovereign and therefore themselves 'undemocratic' is a difficulty that appears originally to have been formulated by Thomas Hobbes, and subsequently inherited by the authors of *The Federalist*, inducing the latter at least to seek to get around it. A great deal of the interest in the theoretical notion of 'balance' probably also reflects the same fear. But this is a matter best developed later in connection with balance, and not here.

The general sort of centralizing argument — for a more efficient and powerful government — advanced by *The Federalist* had been advanced before. It recurs today in the literature promoting, most significantly, European integration and African unity. It is a commonplace for some form of unity to be projected, sometimes rightly, as a means of achieving security, well-being and justice. Not infrequently, as with *The Federalist*, centralizers emerge after a war, and/or in anticipation of war, and this is as characteristic of federalist centralizers as of any others, whether they argue for a union which encompasses a region, a continent or the entire globe. Such was the case with C.H. Saint-Simon (1760–1825), just after the Napoleonic Wars, when he argued for 'the integration of Europe into a single political system while preserving the national independence of each of its peoples'.

Saint-Simon was a centralizing federalist whose position was singular when contrasted with that of other early socialists like William Spence (1750–1814), William Godwin (1756–1836), Robert Owen (1771–1858) and Charles Fourier (1772–1837). These other writers were bound by a common concern to replace the centralized state with a looser union of economic and territorial communes in which the latter would enjoy considerable autonomy (cp. C. Corbo, in Serbyn 1971: 57–83). Saint-Simon, although he shared much of this outlook, none the less argued for a distinctly European parliamentary federation. He reasoned that only an overall political union of the continent — starting with England and France — could inhibit the recurrence of war, lay the foundations for an enduring peace, and thereby generate significant economic development. Saint-Simon's *Réorganisation de la société européenne* (1814) provided an extended treatment of this theme.

Europe is in a violent state. Everybody knows it and says as much
... In any coming together of peoples, as of individuals, common
institutions are obligatory. Without them, only might decides. To
expect to create peace in Europe by treaties and congresses is as
much as imagining that social systems may survive on the mere basis
of convention and agreement. What is required is a compelling force
to unite divergent wills, to concert their activity, to render their
interests common and their commitments firm [Bk. 1, ch. 2].

Saint-Simon provides us here with a centralizing argument which bears
significant affinities to that of *The Federalist*. Both he and 'Publius'
display the mark of Hobbes, which most of us prefer not to see. We
may *note*, too (nothing more), the formal difficulty of employing force
to render force redundant.

J. Hennessy (cp. 1919, 1940, 1942), with less than an echo of Saint-
Simon's acclaim, argued as consistently as any Frenchman or indeed
European for European federation in the period between World Wars I
and II. Hennessy was an army officer during the First War and founded
at the time the *Société Proudhon* with a view to promoting world peace.
Later, he worked with the League of Nations and was for several years
French ambassador to Switzerland. He argued that the Swiss example
demonstrated that federalism alone could reduce the frequency and scale
of war. The ideological content of his federalism was basically derived
from Proudhon, as where the latter argued (in *Du principe fédératif*)
that 'either the twentieth century will initiate a federalist era or human-
ity will endure yet a thousand years more of purgatory'. Proudhon's
contention was that 'a confederate people is a people organized for
peace', which could not fail to be true in the sense that a people who
only act on the basis of agreement and yet sustain a perfectly orderly
rapport can be nothing other than peaceful. Hennessy, however, was
more like Saint-Simon than Proudhon — since Proudhon was really
more interested in a federation of communes than of states, while Saint-
Simon and Hennessy were more concerned with a union of states than
of communes.

Writing in 1941 to Marshal Pétain, the new leader of a defeated and
truncated France, Hennessy (1942) argued that 'the evidence supports
the fact that the German authorities are in no way hostile to the federal
principle and are even prepared to promote it!' (p. 122). He saw federalism as a means of containing the expected advance of the Slavs and
Chinese. He quoted approvingly a Swiss view that 'communism is a
threat to us all' on the assumption that a federally united Europe,

including Hitlerian Germany, would make it possible to contain this
threat. He contended that 'a momentarily defeated France' must re-
sume her role, under Pétain, as a 'great director of peoples' by giving
the green light to federalism (p. 127). Hennessy equated federalism with
neutrality and peace, while still arguing for its great defensive strength
against external dangers. Hitlerian Germany, he contended, presented
no obstacle to peace, since it was not she who first attacked in 1939,
but rather 'England and France who declared war on her' (p. 140). The
United States, given her federal structure, and given that federalism
implied neutrality, should (following Hennessy) have remained neutral
during the war. Hennessy concluded: 'the American abandonment of
the neutrality principle only betrays their infidelity to the underlying
principles of their own federal constitution'. The case that Hennessy
put, tortuous as it was, supported the elaboration of a federal Europe as
a means of achieving integration without force and in order to contain
both internal and external threats of war.

In England, Lionel Curtis (1872-1955) was also a centralizing federalist. At the turn of the century he was actively involved in promoting
South African union. He later argued the cause of an imperial federation which would link Britain with Canada, Australia and New Zealand.
Later still he argued for a world state based on federal union. A London
Times obituary characterized him as 'the most distinguished exponent
in Britain of federalist ideas and of the concept of a world state'. Curtis
was one of several writers, both in this and the last century, who assumed
that all hope for world peace depended upon the construction of a
world state. His argument was that a League of Nations (and implicitly
a United Nations) might represent a step towards peace, but could in no
way guarantee it. He drew a parallel with the first American Confederation and argued expressly that the world must adopt the principles set
out in *The Federalist*. Curtis thought these principles valid now as before, providing in his view the only sure means of securing peace, preserving 'all that is best in nationalism' and attaining 'a higher degree of
freedom' (cp. Curtis 1915, 1934-7, 1945 and 1939). Raymond Silva
(1944) adopted a similar line: 'indeed any imperial system, whose members freely join and whose moral independence is guaranteed, reflects
the federalist idea' (pp. 28-9). So, too, E. Paolini: 'the federal solution
is and remains for Europe and for the world the only one of value' —
committed, as Paolini thinks federalism to be, to peace (in Albertini
1973: 14, 44). A great deal of the support for European integration
— indeed most of it — is federalist, as for example in R. Aron, Daniel
Halévy (see Aron 1958) and Henri Brugmans (1969).

It is difficult to say when a centralizing orientation (federalist or other) 'ought' to be, or 'properly' can be, invoked. Whenever we seek to centralize, that is simply what we seek to do, and whether or not this is the right thing to do must somehow presumably depend upon the concrete reasons we have for seeking such a development at the time we seek it. Centralization in the abstract, and federalism as one of its forms, certainly cannot be regarded as occupying some necessarily privileged moral or mobilizational position. Greater centralization may provide an effective defence against external aggression, but it may also provide an irresistible temptation for engaging in such aggression. It may provide a framework within which associated peoples enjoy peace and prosperity, but it may also permit a given centre to bloodily absorb peoples occupying its periphery. So much depends upon the concrete circumstances that it is difficult to see how any rational person could be committed to the view, abstract or *a priori* in character — even general in character — that centralism is always or usually appropriate, no matter what the cost.

One may attempt to indicate when centralist federalism ought to be *avoided* by stipulating whether, in a given set of circumstances, it enjoys any hope of succeeding (i.e. of becoming a federation). If we are entitled to say that federalism has no hope of succeeding at a given time and place, then we are also entitled to say that federalism is not the proper orientation to invoke in that place and time — on the classic principle that 'ought implies can'. If then we can disengage precise criteria by which to exclude the feasibility of centralist federalism, we shall also have established in this a negative test by which we are permitted to disallow the propriety of such federalism. In principle, there can be no objection to adopting such tests or criteria — should we be able to find them. In practice, the criteria so far adopted have proved trivial.

Riker (1975) holds that for either a European or a world federation to come into being there must exist some 'significant threat', in the absence of which 'there is nothing that will bring such unions about, no matter how much people *wish* for them to happen' (pp. 130-1). For Riker, it is 'naive' to recommend federal union, regionally or globally, simply because there are sound economic and social reasons for it. In addition, he maintains, there must always exist some form of threat, whether external or internal, which the union would serve to overcome. (Riker mentions other criteria but this is for him the crucial criterion, and we are accordingly entitled to pass over the others.) The first point to make, even if far from fatal to Riker, is that those who are most immediately and deeply involved in attempting to construct a European federation are, at the same time, disposed to oppose his analysis in this particular. Brugmans, for example, is quite emphatic that 'if a federal Europe is to come into being, ... it will not be born of Civil War ... , nor generated by an external threat [e.g. the USSR], nor be imposed by an hegemonic power' (1969: 127). This formulation excludes any form of threat as crucial to European integration. Raymond Aron recommends Brugmans as one of those men who has not only fully 'lived' (i.e. experienced), but also lived entirely for, federalism. And there can be no doubt but that in Brugmans's view the federal integration of Europe is – as he puts it – 'an irreversible phenomenon' (p. 99). If Riker is correct in placing the emphasis he does upon the presence of a threat as a prior condition for federal union, then Brugmans can only be 'naive', as Riker puts it, to dismiss this consideration altogether.

Despite the fact that Riker's external threat condition is intuitively attractive, it is none the less imprecise, and the great difficulty accordingly is to formulate it in such a way as to render it less so. There must always be some risk of conflict between states and within them. French Quebec seeks to break away from anglophone Canada; Black America has exploded in revolt against her rulers; terrorism is a diurnal event in Italy and Germany. Basques seek to break away from Spain and France; Northern Ireland is in turmoil. These are facts. And it seems impossible we should be able to travel anywhere without the prospect at least of some *risk* of these things coming about. If such is the case within states, it cannot be necessary to elaborate upon the situation as between them, especially given this century's record of war and rumours of war, together with the continuing and unyielding competition between states, small and large, to equip themselves with ever more powerful engines of destruction. In as far as the risk or threat of conflict is present in all unions whatever, then so must it prove in any specific case of successful federal union. Hence we shall doubtless be able to unearth, retrospectively, some evidence of such a threat should we choose to seek it out. For this sort of excavation to be revealing, however, we should require to know exactly how serious these threats are – in advance of our unearthing them. Riker, unfortunately, does not help us on this point. Thus his 'threat' criterion remains a trivial one. Besides which, even if the criterion were made more precise, it remains that the number of cases we could test (a few dozen at most) is so small, that our results could not possibly enjoy that degree of certainty which Riker would be disposed to accord them.

It is a classic view, expressed by both Hobbes and Locke and shared by many others, that individuals without a common authority over them exist in a state of nature *vis-à-vis* one another. In the case of Hobbes, this 'state of nature' was one of 'Warre'. For Locke, this was not a state of war, but certainly one of partiality, of persons performing as judges in their own case, thus generating injustice, and preparing the ground for further conflict. *The Federalist*, in fact, was disposed to argue a similar position, if indirectly. If the Congress, it contended, were not allowed to control the disposition of the new lands in the West, there would inevitably arise intense competition between the several American states over them. The point was not just that there was a risk of war between the states if they were not united. Rather, because the new states were more proximate both to one another and to the new lands in question, they were, for that reason, more dangerous to one another. The European powers by contrast were relatively remote first in space and thus in the danger they posed. One may infer from *The Federalist* the view that any two independent states (not just individuals) which are competitive and proximate — in some degree all states are — run some risk of war. The arguments for European and for global federation, as advanced by writers as different as Saint-Simon, Hennessy and Curtis, also — in fact primarily — take account of the continuing risk of war between those entities or polities or states which these observers wished to see federated.

We have no difficulty in concluding that, to every state, however small or large, there is always some risk of external war and domestic dissension. This very fact throws some light on the apparently arbitrary way in which Riker sometimes seeks to demonstrate the presence of a 'threat' prior to the achievement of federal union. The conventional view held in relation to the West German federation (cp. e.g. Brugmans 1969: 18) is that the allies imposed it, for good or ill, with a view to splitting up the country after her defeat. (Indeed, this may have been vital to Germany's economic recovery, as Brugmans argues.) Riker, by contrast, feels compelled to argue that post-war Germany, thoroughly broken and devastated as she was, with so much of her territory not only occupied but alienated, became federally centralized (she was in fact decentralized) in response to an external threat. Riker accepts A.H. Birch's argument (1966) that the British-fashioned Nigerian federation of 1960 was, in part, built upon the fear of each of the three regions that the other two would combine against it. Naturally enough, it will be true that there was some external risk to the Germans and some mutual risk (not 'threat') to the Nigerians. But one suspects that some trace of these elements can always be found if one looks hard enough.

In short, it is always possible to play up the case for a threat where a federal entity comes into being, as also to play it down where federation fails. For if a federation is formed from fear of other powers, and formed equally from mutual fear of those states which federate, then virtually any type of fear must provide grounds for federal union. A fear, a threat, may well provide necessary grounds for federal union, but also, perhaps, as argued by Hobbes, for *any* type of union; and it goes without saying that fear and threats also provide grounds for hostility, separation and war.

Any state, given its conjoint attributes of power and independence, always runs the risk and even threat (in as far as this may be both covert and overt) of being obstructed or damaged by parallel entities possessing parallel attributes. It cannot be demonstrated that any two states will always and necessarily perceive one another as threats. But in as far as the notion of a threat runs parallel to that of risk and in this conveys a *potential* threat (as is presupposed by the formula that states have neither permanent friends nor enemies, only permanent interests), it will be clear that the non-perception of a risk or threat cannot be taken as authoritative evidence for its non-existence. This will be all the more obvious where the source of the risk or threat is to be understood as both domestic and foreign. And it is as well to point out that this supposedly two-fold source of risk is in fact three-fold. There may be threats (1) to state A from within (internal dissidence), (2) to state A from state B, and (3) to allied states A and B from state C. *The Federalist* evokes all three of these possibilities – (1) being covered by events like Shays's rebellion in Massachusetts, (2) by the prospect of war between the states for control of the West, and (3) by the prospect of renewed British attack upon the Confederation. It is reasonable to suppose that for any two geographically contiguous states, and even for most which are not, at least some one of these three risk or threat conditions can be met.

It cannot therefore suffice to say that one or more of the three types of risk or threat mentioned above provides a necessary, if not sufficient, condition for the successful inauguration of a federal union. It is like saying that birth is a necessary condition for the flowering of genius. In the one case, as in the other, the condition stipulated is also a condition for failure. To stipulate a condition which is not only necessary for a given development, but also for distinctly opposed or contrary developments, is not very enlightening.

Thus it is true that a threat to state A of internal dissidence may provoke it to federate with state B. But it is equally true that it may inspire it to increase its distance. (Machiavelli in *The Prince* warned rulers against borrowing the troops of their neighbours to quell internal revolt: the lender could so easily thereafter absorb the beneficiary.)

It is true that a threat to state A from state B may provoke federal union between them. In some degree at least, this appears to have occurred in the United States, in Switzerland, and in Nigeria. Such, too, was the federative advice of Saint-Simon to France and England at the close of the Napoleonic Wars, as also of J. Hennessy basically to France and Germany in 1942 following the defeat of the first at the hands of the second. But again, the response of state A might equally well be – in fact it historically more often is – to attempt to increase its distance, by some appropriate means. It was, after all, the threat of the North to the South, both in the USA and in Nigeria, which provoked bloody secessionist attempts, in the USA in the 1860s and in Nigeria in the 1960s. Similarly, despite Saint-Simon's contrary appeal, France very much kept its distance *vis-à-vis* England, and Saint-Simon ran some risk himself in even daring to broach the question of federating with an enemy.

It is true that a threat to states A and B from C may provoke the first two somehow to combine against the third. But it probably more often happens that A or B makes an independent approach to C, especially where C is significantly more powerful than A or B alone, in order to secure some minimal *rapprochement*, the upshot being to deflect hostility (at least for a time) more exclusively towards B or A.

Now we may return to the central point. It is impossible to say in any convincingly universal way, and difficult to say even generally, just when support for a centralizing federalism (or centralization of any kind) is appropriate. Further, it appears equally difficult or impossible to say, universally or generally, when support for such centralizing tendencies is inappropriate and ought to be avoided. Logically, of course, it is pointless to argue for a federalist centralism where it cannot be achieved. The problem is to stipulate, in a non-trivial manner, exactly when that is so. The best that I expect one could do would be to formulate some rather vague and inexact condition permitting or excluding federal union. What is in any event fully evident at the moment is that nothing more precise than this has been accomplished (cp. Davis 1978: 132–3 for a similar criticism of Riker 1964).

We have no clear and probative reason for saying, in any universal way, when exactly we ought to centralize or not (as for example: 'Always' or 'Never'). This conclusion need not stop us from trying to establish the propriety or impropriety of a centralizing ideology, for we must, at some level, decide these matters. None the less, there is some suspicion that the more probative procedure involves less a strict universalist deductivism than an arguing of cases and the provisional establishment of precedents.

So much for federalism as a centralizing ideology. Centralism is not the only federalist ideology. Apart from writers like Henri Brugmans, who are not disposed to consider federalism as an ideology at all, there are others, like A. Herrarte, who would contend that federalism is an *exclusively* centralizing ideology − that 'historically and technically federalism has meant the will to unite, the desire to combine elements that were formerly distinct, the need for cooperation in order to overcome separatist forces' (in Camargo 1972: 269). But this is only half-true. Most informed writers are fully aware − as with C.J. Friedrich, E. McWhinney and S.R. Davis − that federalism may promote decentralism as easily as its opposite.

4 DECENTRALIST FEDERALISM

Just as federalism may represent an argument for centralization, so may it represent an argument for decentralization. Just as the new American federal constitution of 1787 was designed to create a more powerful centre than that provided for by the Articles of Confederation, so the new German federal constitution of 1949 was designed to create a less powerful centre than that provided for under Hitler's Third Reich. There is no 'essential' federalism which any more excludes the one development than the other. And just as the American centralist case involved no argument for absolutism, so the German decentralist case involved no argument for anarchism.

What was achieved in Germany at the instance of an army of occupation (and in some newly independent states under the aegis of British colonial authority) had frequently been promoted in other European states in earlier times by purely domestic elements – if unsuccessfully. C. Hennessy (1962) has written that 'the singularity of the Spaniards [in the nineteenth century] was their equation of republicanism with federalism' (p. xii). The Spanish Revolution of 1868 overthrew Isabella II and occasioned the emergence of the Federal Republican Party, the most celebrated of whose leaders was Pí y Margall (1824–1901). Pí officially led the party from 1870. Later he became president of the Assembly and leader of the country, only to be overturned by a *golpe de estado* in 1874. But the object which Allied powers promoted in a limited and practical way in the German case, Pí y Margall promoted far more broadly, in and out of power, in the case of his native Spain. The difference could be drawn in terms of a contrast between pragmatic and ideological approaches, were it not possible to formulate pragmatism itself as an ideology. Thus it may be better to speak of a contrast between weak and strong ideological forms of decentralist federalism. Of course, it might even be said that the Allied approach was simply 'non-ideological'. But this need create no difficulty as long as we understand 'non-ideological' to be equivalent to 'a *weak* ideological form' of decentralist federalism.

In power, Pí y Margall attempted to carry through a revolution from the top ('una revolución desde arriba') along liberal, socialist and federal lines. He was critical of Proudhon but held him in extraordinarily high esteem, referring to him as the colossus of human reason ('el gigante de

la razón humana') and as the 'Hercules of political economy'. Pí trans-
lated Proudhon's *Du Principe fédératif* (1863) into Spanish in 1868 as
El principio federativo (The Federal Principle), but his most important
book was *La reacción y la revolución* (Reaction and Revolution), published in 1854, and which has been properly described as a forerunner
of the Proudhon book on federalism. Pí's later essay on *La federación*
appeared in 1880. His most recent commentator, Bernaus (1966), reduces all the different facets of the man to an anticlerical, rationalist
liberalism which leads into 'su afirmación de la completa independencia
del individuo' (p. 36) — into a (very Proudhonian) notion of the un-
abridged independence of the individual. As a practical politician, Pí
could not ignore power nor did he decline to take up that which lay
within his reach. None the less, his liberal ideal, like Proudhon's, was
ultimately to eliminate power: 'the creation of a society without power
is the highest of my revolutionary aspirations; it is under the compulsion
of this ultimate end that I determine all subsidiary reforms' (Bernaus:
53). Thus Pí y Margall, this most important of nineteenth-century
Spanish intellectuals, was a striking proponent of federalism as a decentralism, seeing it ultimately as a means of destroying power, but
intermediately as a means of dividing and reducing it. Indeed his was
an anarchist position in the degree that he considered power as nothing
more than a merely temporary, and therefore eliminable, expedient.

In the case of P.-J. Proudhon (1809-65) we encounter another
strong ideological proponent of federation conceived basically as the
perfect institutional reconciliation of liberty and authority. His is a
deceptive theory of balance (most theories of balance *are* deceptive)
which reduces basically to an *a priori* decentralism. His claims, in *Du
Principe fédératif*, are uninhibited: 'Among so many systems of government which philosophy proposes and which history tests, the only one
which combines the individually and socially indispensable features of
justice, order, liberty and stability is . . . federalism' (p. 20). Proudhon's
claim is that 'every state is by nature expansionist' with the exception
of federations ('il en est autrement dans le système fédératif'). Being
largely consistent in this abstract outlook, Proudhon deduced that a
world government of a *federal* kind was merely illogical. He thought
Europe itself much too large for any single federation — one could only
build 'a federation of federations'. (Proudhon uses the expressions
'federation' and 'confederation' interchangeably.) Basically, he wanted
to start by decentralizing all European states, somehow thereby to
achieve a general disarmament, and 'reduce all nationality to liberty'
(pp. 86-90). In this case it is plain that Proudhon's chief emphasis was

upon decentralism, that he was ideologically committed to it, and that he promoted it in the strong or universal sense, and not in any limited, halting or pragmatic way. The reason for all of this, at least logically, is that Proudhon's outlook was dramatically unilinear. In effect, he reveals a prior and perhaps exclusive commitment to a single value – liberty. Federation, as he put it, is 'Liberty', and 'excludes any idea of constraint' (p. 85).

Proudhon's federalism bears only a superficial resemblance to that of Saint-Simon. Saint-Simon took the state for granted, and assumed that existing state entities should amalgamate, on the assumption that the emasculation of sovereign independence would inhibit the animal urge to war that was a part of the nature of independence *per se*. Proudhon, unlike Saint-Simon, did not take the state for granted, but basically regarded it as evil incarnate; and far from seeking as a top priority to amalgamate European states in their present form, he put domestic reform first, reform involving several varieties of decentralization. Proudhon then was not so much disposed to espouse federalism as a means of securing common defence, or as a means of establishing larger and more powerful governments, but rather as a means of promoting individual liberty. Formally, Proudhon was concerned with larger state entities, as built from the bottom up. But, practically, in order to achieve this result, it was first necessary to decentralize – as Pí y Margall intended – from the top down, within each existing state. It is this orientation, and the primacy of this orientation, which converts Proudhon chiefly into a proponent of decentralist federalism.

The position with Michael Bakunin (1814-76) was much the same as with Proudhon. Liberty he perceived as the end of socialism and socialism as a means to liberty. Proudhon's federalism was derived from the notion of contract, as a voluntary mutual exchange of a measure of independence against some matching and mutual advantage. Bakunin's federalism also builds from the bottom up, from commune to nation and beyond, with each freely contracting association arising from that beneath it. The whole, as Bakunin conceived it, would culminate in a universal federation of peoples – a global entity. Such federalism, for Bakunin, constituted the political framework of socialist anarchism (cp. Bakunin 1953: 271-6 and C. Carbo in Serbyn 1971: 57-83). Again, the reader may be distracted by the notion of building from the bottom up, suggesting a centralist orientation. The fact is, that in the view of Proudhon, and more especially of Bakunin, no decentralized bottom existed to be built upon. The primary objective therefore would be to bring this base into being – and this orientation locates the essential character of a decentralist ideology.

Too much may be made of the general identity between the views of Bakunin and those of Proudhon. Although they knew one another and shared common views and interests, it remains that Proudhon usually appeared more radical and Bakunin more moderate than either in fact was. Proudhon in effect defended property, inheritance of property and non-violence, while opposing global federation. By contrast, Bakunin unabashedly celebrated violent revolution and class war, while supporting global federation. None the less, as Eugene Pyziur (1955) has written,

> Bakunin was undoubtedly indebted to Proudhon for his rejection of the phenomenon of authority and of the institution of the state. Proudhon, more than any other, was responsible for transforming Bakunin's instinctive revolt against authority into a conscious anarchist creed . . . This adoption of Proudhon's ideas was of fundamental importance, since the rejection of any legal authority is the starting point for the entire anarchist doctrine [p. 39].

And although there may be some doubt, as Pyziur noted, about the indebtedness of Bakunin to Proudhon for his federalist ideas, it remains that there is a substantive similarity between them.

The 'main task which Bakunin assigned to . . . federalism', as Pyziur wrote, 'was that of so parcelling out political power that the result would be the total annihilation of the state and of all political domination and power' (p. 131). Every individual, commune, province and state was to enjoy an inalienable right to secede from the larger entity to which it belonged. This orientation stems from Bakunin's commitment to the view that − in his own words − 'no value exists outside freedom'. This, of course, is a conventional liberal view, and starting from it, liberals (like Tocqueville and Acton) traditionally regarded power as a 'necessary evil'. Bakunin was aware of the logic of this idea, and tried to distance himself from it. Pyziur (p. 115), for one, was persuaded of Bakunin's success in securing the distinction between the anarchist concept of liberty and the liberal notion of individualism. But only a partially satisfactory case of this kind can be made. There is a difference between liberalism and anarchism in as far as Bakunin's anarchism rejects the liberal view that individual liberty somehow exists prior to society itself. (Bakunin's view is more evolutionary and materialistic in that it takes liberty to be a product of society, rather than society − as in the Social Contract theory − to be a product of liberty.) But, beyond this purely historical consideration, no further difference of import is to be noted. Whether or not liberty historically evolved from a social condition, the chief question that arises is how an 'absolute right' to be guided by one's own will and to be responsible to one's self alone is compatible with the preservation of social arrangements, including the state, which nowhere — as far as we know — entirely correspond to what every member or citizen would freely agree with. If, as for Bakunin, any limitation upon freedom is 'domination', it is difficult to see how the continued existence of either society or state can prove compatible with the full realization of liberty. This is a problem confronted by both liberalism and anarchism.

Peter Kropotkin (1842-1921) offers us a variety of decentralist federalism which is neither systematic nor easily distinguished from the similar views expounded by Proudhon and Bakunin. His major concern was to break up highly centralized parliamentary regimes. He rejected the hierarchical views of Saint-Simon but was strongly attracted to the decentralist federalism of figures like Fourier and Proudhon. Berneri (1976) rightly suggested in 1922 that 'one of the most interesting aspects of Kropotkin's political thought is the federalist idea which constantly recurs in his writings and which forms one of the basic factors in his anarchist ideology'. Although Kropotkin lived out his final days as a figure of some prestige in the country north of Moscow under the new Bolshevik regime — once being courted by Lenin himself — it remains that he died a greatly disappointed man. What he had hoped for was a federal structure wildly different from that achieved by the new Soviet state. The chief purpose of Kropotkin's federalism was to secure a decentralization of power to the local, communal level, rather than the concentration of all significant initiatives at the centre (cp. Kropotkin 1885, 1886, 1892, 1898 and 1902; Woodcock and Avakumović 1950: 453-4). We shall have occasion to return to Kropotkin for more critical inspection.

For figures like Pí y Margall, Proudhon, Bakunin and Kropotkin, federalism was an expression of particularity, individualism, democracy. For these men, federal institutions were taken as a means of realizing such ideals, of inhibiting the growth of power, even as a means ('on balance') of destroying power. Other proponents of federalism, such as Tocqueville, John Calhoun, James Bryce, Edward Freeman, Gierke, Figgis, Krabbe, the early Laski and Sobei Mogi, were prejudiced in favor of an *a priori* decentralism, but simultaneously and consciously resisted the clear, anarchical implications of such an orientation, thus accepting some notion of 'balance' as the solution, one frequently conceived as an ideal. This species of strong and principled commitment to federalism as a balance between centralism and decentralism survives, even lustily, into the present (cp. Voyenne 1976: 8).

The formal promotion of federalism as a political philosophy of 'balance' is normally incoherent or unstable. On the theoretical level, it may translate out as an argument either for more centralization or for more decentralization. On the practical level, the effect can be equally ambivalent. The fact is that talk of balance is a rhetorical device, too often difficult to resist. If one seeks either greater centralization or greater decentralization, it is tempting to do so in such a way as to suggest that what one seeks is not novel, but normal; not absurd, but sound; and one may invoke the metaphor of 'balance' to achieve that effect. Proudhon, for example, formally argued for a balance between liberty and authority and identified federalism as the embodiment of this balance. But the whole thrust of his formal analysis, if not necessarily of his practical intention, was to secure a decentralist federalism of an anarchist type. In the United States, the chief proponent of decentralist federalism was John Calhoun (1782–1850), who argued for a theoretical balance, for a countervailing power. But Calhoun was practically concerned to further entrench local power – in this case, the power of a rural, slave-holding South. While Proudhon's analysis in effect pointed towards an *a priori* decentralism of an anarchist type, Calhoun's merely pointed towards such further decentralization as would safeguard the power of a particular oligarchy.

It has already been indicated that the basic thrust of *The Federalist* is centralist; the work is marked by the imprint of the sovereignty doctrine, but falls well short of an *a priori* or absolutist centralism. There is no comparably elaborate and seminal discussion of the Bonn constitution. But Calhoun's argument, advanced a century earlier, and like the Bonn Basic Law in outline, was American; both sought to strengthen the periphery against the centre; both reflect a fundamental distrust of an unadulterated sovereignty; both equally reject any concept of anarchism. While we are entitled to regard the thrust of *The Federalist* as centralist, and that of the Bonn Basic Law and of Calhoun's *A Disquisition on Government* as decentralist, they can all equally be read, if we wish it so, as expressions of 'balance'. It is only necessary to note the greatly divergent forms that any 'balance', so understood, can assume. This concern with balance, however, cannot be appropriately developed at this juncture. Calhoun (1851) provided a federalism which was explicitly shorn of the anarchist inclination (if not implication) found in those decentralist writers earlier cited.

There are at least two significant or strong types of ideological statement we could make about decentralist federalism — first, that decentralism is universally desirable, and thus always to be promoted; and secondly, that it is only generally desirable, and thus ought usually (perhaps 'most times' and not just 'sometimes') to be promoted. The universal statement is the more interesting because of its combined sweep and precision. The generalization, by contrast with the universalization, reveals no clear principle. A centralization of power implies that some decisions (as to do with the compulsory schooling of children) are reserved to some numerically more restricted plural or single agent (such as a local authority rather than a multitude of parents), and that this more uniform and concentrated power of decision displaces the earlier, more multiform and disparate decisions, while retaining the same binding effect of the previous decisions upon the objects or matters being decided. A decentralization of power, by contrast, implies that the number of agents taking a decision is increased rather than restricted. If one recommends this inverse movement universally, one is recommending that decisions to be taken *for* other agents should increasingly be taken *by* them. The terminus of such movement, logically, can only be a very strict individualism and socio-political anarchy. Of course, many decisions which we take for others may be nefarious, as when we decide to banish, imprison, torture or electrocute folk; but they may also be benign, as where we educate, entertain, rescue or reconcile them. Naturally, too, we may take decisions for others with and without their consent. Often we certainly believe we have no choice but to take decisions without the express consent of those for whom they are taken: some individuals may be rescued who clearly prefer to drown; others we may compel to remain in school when they would undoubtedly prefer to be at play in the street; others still we may insist upon disarming despite an evidently heartfelt desire on their part to ventilate unloved ones. A universally decentralist ideology, as we can see, would run counter to any such decision-making (*for* others), whether we choose sweetly to call it 'authoritative' or, more harshly, 'authoritarian'. It is in this sense that one is disposed to maintain that anarchism, together with a universally decentralist federalism (such federalism, in truth, reducing to political anarchism), is basically unacceptable.

The most sweeping justification of anarchism — that is of an *a priori* decentralism and individualism — is that full human accord is possible and can be achieved by giving full rein either to our instincts or to reason (or to both), thereby excluding the play of force, together with all other arbitrary means of achieving human accord. Peter Kropotkin's assumption was that the primary aim was less to achieve such accord than to secure total human self-realization. He urged his readers to 'be great', to 'be strong', to develop their lives in every direction — physically and intellectually — to venture even into danger ('for danger has its own great pleasures'), to 'jump into the water that we may save, not a human being only, but even a cat' (Kropotkin 1892: 33-4). In all of this, Kropotkin, as he thought, was paraphrasing the system of ethics expounded by Jean Marie Guyau. (Kropotkin mistakenly referred to him as Marc, rather than Jean Marie.) Guyau argued for the termination of all forms of moral absolutism, together with the institutionalized punishment associated with it. His assumption was that one can discover no genuinely universal moral principle in nature, reason or faith; that in as far as there is or can be no universally binding principle, there can be no genuine ethical obligation either (i.e. of an absolute and invariable kind); and that without an invariable moral rule to apply, it cannot be proper to impose sanctions either — one would be punishing offenders for the breach, in effect, of a non-existent rule. In sum, Guyau thought 'it is impossible to systematize the various hypotheses which men may devise about the proper nature of their conduct and convert them all into a single metaphysical ethic to be imposed universally upon human reason' (Guyau 1885: 225). To assume that there is only one correct ethical or political norm, and to punish people for not conforming to it, was for Kropotkin irreducibly tyrannical. His essential concern was for the individual to flourish. Kropotkin's chief means to this was negative — consisting in destroying the government or whatever else obstructed the end. For Kropotkin it was less the case that government restrains, than that it generates, criminality — on the assumption that its basic aim is to defend social inequity, and that it employs punishment to brutalize the least fortunate so as to keep them in line. The implication is that to reduce government will *pro tanto* reduce crime (which, in different senses, is both true and false) and that all mechanisms of non-voluntary social control should be removed (a far more doubtful proposition).

The basic counter-argument to the overarching anarchist view is to the effect that human variability and individuality — in commitment, specialization, intelligence and so on — are far too great to permit any automatic accord of either a rational or instinctive kind. Behaviour which we qualify as instinctive may be narrowly or broadly identified. If broadly identified (as where a writer suggests that war is an outcome of a territorial drive), then by saying too much one explains too little. If narrowly identified (as where one maintains that humans always attempt to preserve themselves), then the specification easily permits us to locate myriad exceptions. It is not static human differences that matter — as of age, weight, IQ, etc. — but the dynamic behavioural differences which the former may signal, in relation to both the formulation and implementation of a common set of rules. Humans do not all agree, nor appear to have any rational or instinctive means of securing entire agreement, on the common rules by which they shall be bound. Even if the basis of human accord is instinctual, it is clear that such a 'basis' is inadequate. Rational reflection is certainly important, and yet the necessary limitations of time always mean that debate on any matter to be decided (at some fixed point in time) must always (at some antecedent point in time) be foreclosed. Thus the devising or eliciting of common rules — as well as their implementation — always appears to be characterized by some element of arbitrariness. There seems to be no certain way by which any of us individually or collectively may alight upon the right and the good. Even were such rules abstractly possible and concretely available it appears certain that we would not all of us either agree to them or interpret them uniformly. Indeed, as the world becomes smaller, and technologically more sophisticated, the citizens of every nation are increasingly trained in ever more divergent fields, and appear to nourish, in fact and potentially, correspondingly more divergent sub-national mentalities and psychologies, even as this process creates broad rules regulating their traffic with the citizens of other lands.

By contrast with all this, it is clear that all members of any human community are, at various points, dependent (as for example children, cripples, students, etc.) or interdependent (as for example urban workers and rural farmers). Dependence and interdependence are constraints that are always with us and it is these constraints which argue for — 'compel' would not be too strong a word — convergence. Were there no constraints upon us, it is almost certain that highly personal and variegated 'rules' would flourish with all the extravagance of hothouse plants. Children, in growing up, diverge from parental models. Philosophers, following the demise of their mentors, alter received teachings. Settlers, at one remove from their ancestral homes, evolve and adopt novel political systems. Individuals, once in power, perform in a manner distinct from that anticipated when they were not in power. In all cases, to remove a constraint is to invite novelty. Such innovation may be desirable; it may be innocuously aesthetic or metaphysical. But divergence also has its practical side. It is as natural for individuals, left alone, to devise different moral rules as to fashion different types of clay pot. The trouble is that we can cope with, and even indeed welcome, different types of material artifice, but cannot with equal ease accept conflicting rules about 'correct' social and political behaviour. Conflicts between rules have a way of translating out as conflicts over things, as where a native population reveres and seeks to retain all ancestral land, whether tilled or not, in contrast to the expansionist settler who will justify the appropriation of any land by those who will render it productive. Two such rules, and two populations so ruled, will not achieve community in peace.

Given that human differences, where formulated as divergent evaluative and behavioural rules, are likely at many points to lead into conflict, the problem is to determine how best to contain such conflict. One might question whether it were better to do nothing at all. Perhaps the first point to accept is that conflict can never be completely contained — that every potentially controlling agent is limited, that every relevant controlling procedure will have disadvantages as well as advantages, and that every attempt to contain conflict may carry some risk of extending it. But just as intervention does not necessarily guarantee peace, neither will non-intervention necessarily do so. If, however, doing nothing on occasion generates peace — two rival chiefs may decline to intervene so as not to enlarge a war and so bring it to an early end — then 'doing nothing' must be re-interpreted as a sub-category of 'doing something'. The relevant contrast is not in this sense, therefore, between doing something and doing nothing but between doing something and doing everything: complete containment of conflict is not a possibility, and just as it is excluded in practice, so should it be in theory. It is in this most important sense that anarchism is a mistaken theory — where it suggests that doing nothing is not to do something. If we do not set up an army or police force, it does not necessarily mean that no force, whether that of a bully or a battalion, will predominate. If we do institute some such force — which is today what always happens — then we must recognize that the effect cannot possibly be either, on the one side, to eliminate force as such or, on the other, to secure that an actual 'monopoly' of coercive power is established within the system. The centre that is said to enjoy a 'monopoly' of coercive power is merely one which has achieved enough of an edge over other possible centres of resistance — those distinctly recognized as such — to be able usually to triumph over them, singly or collectively, in case of conflict. The trouble is, of course, that many potential centres of resistance are often not recognized as such, and the centre thought to enjoy a power 'monopoly' is frequently seen, where conflict supervenes, to enjoy nothing of the kind. The 'paradox' of the urge to secure a power monopoly is that the further a given centre moves in this direction, the further is it likely to move in the opposite direction; for the more 'certain' the monopoly that accrues to a given centre, the more firmly hostile towards it will other elements in the system become. In sum, not to have a formal army or police force is not the same as having no force at all. And to have some force, formal or not, is not the same as being unfair or unjust.

One may try, with little prospect of success, to impose in advance a common rule upon every aspect of social and political life. Such, indeed, appears to be the object of a fully ideological absolutism, an unyielding centralism, which seeks a single principle to encompass every difficulty. Just as one may appeal for one rule and one centre to remove all conflict, so may one appeal, not just for the bare negation of this demand, but for a permanent and unending decentralization of control to achieve the same result. The prospect of success is as pockmarked and emaciated a creature in the one case as in the other. Just as one cannot say, confronting difference, 'Always impose a common policy', neither can one say, 'Never do so'. The question impliedly being asked is whether we should ever *impose* a common rule or policy – and, if so, when. The opposed responses, 'Yes, Always' and 'No, Never', are of course extremes. In between are to be found many other contending possibilities. Assuming that we take neither extreme (it is not clear that there is a 'middle' position), we might advise imposition whenever a majority (minimal or maximal) consents; or only when there is prior *unanimous* agreement that a more minimal majority may be invoked; or at any time the system is 'fundamentally' threatened, irrespective of any head-counting; or when a dominant elite or an enlightened despot says so; and so on. But the only significant option being canvassed by *a priori* decentralism, or anarchism – which is the present object of concern – has to do with the notion that a common policy should *never* be imposed.

The fundamental question is really whether, having agreed total non-imposition as a policy, we could ever carry it out. We must assume from the start that not everyone will agree that *no* common policy should ever be imposed. This rules out the prospect of any national or global unanimity on such a matter. Assume then that a vote is taken, whether grandly plebiscitary or meanly parliamentary. Those who support the non-imposition policy, confronted with those who oppose it, will either be overridden or themselves override their opponents. If the non-impositionists allow themselves to be overridden, then they acquiesce in an imposition which it was their *raison d'être* to oppose. If, by contrast, they override the opposition, then they impose the precise outcome which it was their original intention to avoid. It accordingly appears to be the case that, even if a group of deciders decide never to impose nor allow to be imposed a common policy where such a policy is not fully agreed by all who would be affected by it, such an agreement, in one way or another, will fail in its object. In other words, the imposition of *some* communality is a circumstance which it is difficult to conceive as altogether avoidable. (This need not prevent one from claiming, with the anarchists, that *most* common rules neither are nor need be imposed – certainly not by force.) In as far as anarchism seeks to avert all imposed communality, then it wears a somewhat improbable (if fetching) habit.

If this broad counter-argument to an *a priori* doctrine of decentralism is telling, then it will have the effect of inhibiting the urge to embrace such an anarchist doctrine. But not because the argument has killed the doctrine. After all, if we are told we must always centralize, or by contrast always decentralize, we are being told at least two things, the first being what to do in future and the second being that the doing of it is possible. It would appear to be just as difficult to demonstrate that, in the future, political life cannot be absolutely centralized, as to demonstrate, for the future, that society will be quite unable to function unless there is some authoritative and uninvited decision-making of some for others. We may rule out the feasibility of absolutist and anarchist contingencies by reference to present knowledge and reasoning. But the underlying human reality may change; alternatively our knowledge of it may simply expand, and what at one point appears impossible may at another appear otherwise.

Whether or not a doctrine of decentralist federalism, or of political anarchism, proves impossible, improbable or just unacceptable, the doctrine must be distinguished from the programme. There is not always, perhaps never, a neat fit between abstract doctrines and concrete programmes. There is always the inevitable gap between aim and reach. But this is not at all the distinction being presently considered. There is always, too, some conflict between distinct universals (as between selflessness and self-preservation, or even between liberty and authority) *qua* universals. The effect of such conflict is that its component terms cannot in any very obvious way be rationally reconciled. The Kantian, naturally, may insist that the absoluteness of these individual terms persists, even when mutually repugnant. But it is difficult to see how any two principles (such as liberty/authority) can each be universally valid if it is simultaneously accepted that each term contradicts the other. In a way, this is not even an interesting problem; more relevantly, it still does not quite reflect the distinction intended as between doctrine and programme. What we are really concerned with is the simple difference between those specific changes which agents may concretely seek in a given time and place, by contrast with their inclination to identify such change as implicit in or deducible from a given principle, doctrine or ideology. For example, one might promote the replacement of a criminal justice system inspired by vengeance (retribution) with a system where the imposition of restraints upon offenders was legitimated solely by reference to the deterrent effect of such restraints (i.e. their capacity to protect society against the recurrence of certain categories of undesirable behaviour). This concrete desire for change (as sought for example by Guyau) could be *regarded* as implicit in and deducible from a great variety of principles and doctrines — whether liberty, equality, democracy, socialism, anarchism or other. What is characteristic, however, is the fact that the concrete programme appears to accommodate itself to rival principles, doctrines or ideologies. This situation suggests that the relationship between the programme and the principle is in large part fortuitous. Put simply and summarily, there is much in the programme of decentralist federalism, taken as a political anarchism, which many folk, including the author, find genuinely engaging and desirable. If we distinguish this acceptance, however, from an *a priori* decentralist principle, we need encounter no difficulty in simultaneously rejecting the latter as circular, closed, unarguable and irrational.

It appears likely (although it is difficult to see how the matter might be tested) that a decentralist federalism seems attractive to so many precisely because of its programmatic, if not its doctrinal, content. Kropotkin, for example, may well have imagined that authority and centralization are evil, and that the only way, or at least the chief means, of overcoming the difficulty (and incidentally achieving communism) lies in 'the abolition of the state, by the conquest of complete individual liberty, by mutual accord, by modes of association and federation which are entirely free' (Kropotkin 1896: 32). But more concretely than his concern with abolishing the state and securing complete liberty might suggest, Kropotkin was practically concerned with reducing and, as far as possible, eliminating the use of physical force as a means of social control. One need only note that the ideal of total freedom is one thing; the concrete concern with significantly inhibiting the use of force is quite another.

Kropotkin took the view that there were three basic means of achieving social control. The first and worst was force. The second and most ineffective was by preaching and moralizing. The third and most important was the practice and example of mutual aid. The clue to his practical programme lies less in what he positively promoted than in those social practices he sought to undermine. The central practice to be overturned was the institutionalization of force. For Kropotkin, the position was not that humans are better than we know them to be, but that brutalizing them only makes them worse than they can become. Kropotkin continually argued that the bulk of violations of law — by those highly placed — are never punished anyway; that the bulk of those who are punished are merely folk who are too poor and powerless to avoid the evil; that for more powerful offenders to secure that evil is inflicted upon the less powerful is grossly corrupt, and so on. Again, Kropotkin leaped from this successful attack to the odd conclusion that the entire system must be destroyed. But to sanction the destruction of a system may require sanctioning some use of force to bring it off. In fact, Kropotkin appears to have believed that it *must* do so. Being caught in this bind — that is force is an evil which cannot be destroyed without force — he felt called upon obliquely to defend force as supportive of a good cause by contrast with that force which serves an evil purpose. He urged his readers not to complain too much about nasty anarchist violence. The perpetrators of such evil, after all, were only using against the more powerful the evil which the latter have at all times visited upon the powerless. In any event, for Kropotkin, these gross and violent habits were inculcated by the system itself, suggesting that when we complain about anarchist violence as internally inconsistent we should — again — blame the system (cp. Kropotkin 1886, 1896)!

Despite this brisk gavotte, Kropotkin still suffered from a spot of gout. For it is one thing to say that force is evil *per se*, and another entirely contradictory thing to suggest that some of it has to be lived with — that it is (however minimally) acceptable. (The problem is exactly parallel to that faced by the liberal for whom liberty is the only value but who succumbs to the temptation to restrict it — in the interest of greater liberty!) There are at least two ways in which Kropotkin might have got round the difficulty. First, he might merely have toned down the initial objection to force, to say something to the effect that in practice it is usually evil, for being unnecessary or excessive or irrelevant, and that in all such cases its use should be opposed, and even (where required) by sufficient force to check the evil. Secondly, and alternatively, he might just have stuck to his guns, holding force to be evil, and opposing any use of violence to check violence as an increase of evil, not a diminution of it. (He actually advances this argument where it relates to social or institutional force but retreats from it in the discussion of and muted apologia for revolutionary violence.) The effect of the first gambit would be to retreat from the characterization, express or implicit, of force as bedrock evil beyond all contestation. The effect of the second opening would be to accept the improbability of any total prohibition on the use of force, in view of the absence of any operational plan for checking it. Of course, Kropotkin could have promulgated an operational plan of a non-violent kind along the lines first espoused by Mahatma Gandhi in India and subsequently by Martin Luther King in the Southern states of America. But if he had done this, his position presumably would have been more that of a gradualist than a revolutionist — that is it could no longer have been the position of a man who sought, at least formally, to destroy the system as a whole. Even if Kropotkin (or any similar anarchist or federalist) were to accept a non-violent stance as an operational means, together with its attendant piecemeal and gradualist approach — which is often an effective and sensible position to adopt — it does not follow that the promotion of non-violence intended by such tactics will in fact be achieved. Actually, the reverse of the express intention may out. The reason is that non-violence, although a very great deal can be said for it situationally, may place less of a check upon violence than hold out to it an object to feed upon (as in the case of acquiescence to extermination within the Nazi camps of the Second World War).

In summary, the chief difficulty with Kropotkin (and with *a priori* decentralism generally) relates to an exaggerated statement of principle conjoined with the inclination to wink at violations of the principle when these violations are displayed by one's own side. It would perhaps have sufficed for Kropotkin to say that force in practice, where unnecessary or excessive or irrelevant (it seems usually to be at least one of these), is evil and requires (where so understood) to be opposed. We are not prevented from accepting, where we recognize the *a priori* decentralist doctrine to be unconvincing, that much of the programme practically associated with it was both sound and intensely humane. *A priori* decentralism proposes to tell us in a simple and universal way when we should decentralize — which is now and always. The doctrine is not convincing, first because of its logical circularity, and secondly because it conflicts — given our present stage of global development — with so many other values (associated with the complexity and relative sophistication of the modern world) which we either cherish or cannot wholly turn round for fear of compounding our difficulties.

A consistently held, universally decentralist doctrine is possibly 'impossible'. But this is not an 'impossibility' one could ever properly demonstrate. Anarchism calls for a state of affairs where no one takes any decisions of a kind which affects others in a way that these dislike or disapprove. And there is no way that we can insist – empirically, and in advance of the evidence, scattered as this will be across an infinity of future experience – that such a situation simply cannot come about. There are many good reasons for thinking such an anarchism will not come about. There are also reasons for considering that it would be unfortunate if it did (consider the difficulty or impossibility of rearing children, the great loss of time among adults, the almost inescapable reversion to a system of subsistence production, and so on). But we cannot actually demonstrate it to be impossible. Indeed, one conceivably could carry on decentralizing, spreading authority, *ad infinitum* – just as historically we have carried on centralizing – even if it produced a massive drop in human reproduction, an extraordinary dispersal of the population that remained, and even if that population only survived for one generation more.

Decentralist federalism – and the autonomy of local, territorial communities which it promotes – is sometimes upheld on the grounds that such autonomy is desirable in itself. The trouble is that local, territorial autonomy may easily prejudice the rights of other groups or interests (especially where these form less than a majority) within the local community in question. Local decentralization can only go so far, and wherever it stops it will not be short of confirming some ethnic, class, racial, sexual or other group in an underrepresented or minoritarian position. In brief, we cannot be sure that federalist or any other decentralism will do more than protect the interests of that sub-section of the overall community which controls or dominates the locality. To protect local, territorial rights may easily conflict with the protection of the rights of minorities resident in the locality. An example of this sort may be taken from West Germany.

In 1957, the supreme court or *Bundesverfassungsgericht* sided with the province or *Land* of Niedersachsen and against the federal government or *Bundesrepublik* in the *Reichskonkordat* case. Niedersachsen, with a Protestant majority, insisted upon compulsory non-religious education for all students within its territory. The federal government argued that Catholics in Niedersachsen should be permitted to retain their own schools – which would appear perfectly reasonable – but on the rather remarkable grounds that only a foreign treaty (the German-Vatican Concordat of 1933) bound the state of Niedersachsen to permit such an indulgence. Given so irrelevant an argument, the court was perhaps more than entitled to overrule the federal government in this

.matter. But the effect was simultaneously to defend the autonomy of a local government while denying a Catholic minority the right to its own religious schools (cp. McWhinney 1965: 64ff).

In as far as political error — 'evil' might not prove too strong an expression — is perceived in terms of the possession of a certain 'quantum' of power, the corrective may be perceived in equally inappropriate, quantitative terms: as the diffusion of this quantum. If we take decentralist federalism as an abstract goal, it will be clear that, on its own, it is insufficient to secure perfect democracy or approximate justice or even great efficiency. These desired outcomes may often be helped along by decentralist federalism, but it does not automatically secure them. Entrenched local control may well further representative government, participatory democracy, human rights, 'due process' of law, responsible leadership and so forth. But there are myriad examples, as in the Southern United States and southern Italy, where for centuries this was not and is not so. The power accorded to a local oligarchy to rule, whatever its description, will always in some degree permit it to deal unfairly, sometimes grossly so, with those subject to it and most especially where the latter take no part in, or are automatically denied any significant impact upon, local deliberations. The moral propriety of decentralist federalism, then, cannot be determined unless or until due account is taken of whether — and also of the manner and degree in which — such territorial decentralization prejudices the rights and interests either of non-majoritarian or non-dominant elements within the locality.

5 FEDERALIST BALANCE

Many observers have conceived federalism as representing a balance. Proudhon embraced it as an ideal of balance between liberty and authority. Alexandre Marc has more recently celebrated it as 'la diversité dans l'unité'. Bernard Voyenne has recommended it, less crisply, as a 'dialectically complementary' relationship between 'autonomy and participation', as a resolution of the human aspiration simultaneously for independence and solidarity. R.L. Watts (1966) has argued that federal societies are distinguished by 'the relative balance of demands for integration and diversification', by 'an approximate equilibrium between ... wider and narrower nationalisms', where the forces of neither unity nor diversity predominate. The notion of balance, taken to imply an equilibrium between opposed forces, is popularly associated with, if not logically tied to, the idea of 'give and take', which may lead, by extension, to notions of compromise. Henri Brugmans has pinned compromise to federalism as its highest badge of honour; he extols federalism as integrating without absorbing, as joining communities that are dissimilar and yet allied, as increasing common power while preserving traditional liberties. André Bernard reflects a nearly identical commitment (in Serbyn 1971). But Edward Freeman (1863) wrote long ago of federal government as being 'in its essence, a compromise between two opposite political systems'.

These notions of balance and compromise are in turn linked — explicitly or implicitly — to a view of federalism as a form of contractual arrangement. Here federalism is regarded as a *foedus*, a pact (deriving from *fides* or trust) implying an agreement that is freely and mutually consented to, whereby each party surrenders a degree of autonomy in exchange for some compensating advantage. It is in this concrete sense that Carl Friedrich (1974) abstractly maintains that 'we can properly speak of federalism only if a set of political groupings coexist and interact as autonomous entities, united in a common order with an autonomy of its own'. Contract theory, however, may promote distinct varieties of purpose, and so, too, federalism, when contractually conceived. Contract theory may serve to bolster and to justify authority, as when one suggests that an agent has freely agreed a certain principle or arrangement and is accordingly bound to comply with some implication or rule derived from it. Alternatively, contract may be employed to justify disobedience, as when one suggests that some established authority has either exceeded its mandate or violated agreed rules which it was committed to obey, thereby voiding its authority. In other words, the ethical and ideological effect of contract theory may be to encourage either compliance or non-compliance, either authority or liberty. As I have argued elsewhere, 'contract theory, applied deductively, could be made to justify (1) virtually any tyrannical act on the part of government and (2) tolerance of any licentious act on the part of citizens' (1967: 119–29). Federalism, conceived as a *foedus*, or contract, may similarly encourage greater centralism (as did *The Federalist*) or greater decentralism (as did the Bonn 'Constitution' or Basic Law of 1949). An ideology of balance, however, promotes neither liberty nor authority, neither centralism nor decentralism, but both conjointly. The difficulty is that where we promote 'balance', 'compromise', 'contractualism' as such – and indeed federalism so conceived – then we find that we do not lend ourselves to an ethical or ideological notion which is altogether perspicuous. Any power relationship at all, even that between master and slave, involves some give and take, some reciprocity, even compromise, all of which can be reinterpreted in terms of 'balance' or 'contractualism'. The only difference is that contract implies consent and that balance implies equilibrium. As for consent, there is virtually no social practice in which an individual is engaged to which he cannot be said to have consented. (The classical justification of slavery, as echoed by many, like Hobbes and Grotius, was contractual: the conquered swore total fealty to the conqueror in exchange for life.) As for balance, it is merely a metaphor for 'right' or 'just'; accordingly, any unequal or imbalanced relationship (especially of power) can be referred to as 'balanced', as long as we approve of it.

The theory of social contract has been variably expounded by a great range of writers, such as Languet (1581), Mariana (1599), Althusius (1603), Suarez (1613), Grotius (1625), Hobbes (1651), Pufendorf (1672), Locke (1690), Rousseau (1762), Proudhon (1863), Renouvier (1869) and Spencer (1884). It was employed, too, by Fichte and Kant and in our own day it has been revived in a novel manner by John Rawls. The history of the theory in modern times starts in the sixteenth century (cp. Gough 1957). It does not first appear as a social contract and subsequently as a contract of government. As is well known, the order of appearance is reversed. It is only the later theory of a *social* contract (as advanced by figures like Hobbes and Rousseau) which presupposes a state of nature composed of individuals – who are compelled to transmute their chaotic individuality into a coherent communality.

Earlier social-contract theory by contrast took the social order for granted and did no more than posit the specific emergence of institutions of government from it.

All theories of contract cannot be decisively sorted out into social and governmental categories, nor can all contract theorists be simply described as proponents of one or the other orientation. Locke, for example, employed both. Federalism can also be said to repose upon both theories of contract. In contract theory, whether governmental or social, one begins either from an individual, or from a group, who represents or constitutes certain interests. If the contractors are groups, the assumption must be that certain rights naturally attach to these groups (as for example, churches or families or corporations or regions) and that the established government has a duty to protect these group rights (most essentially to survival, but also perhaps to property, etc.). If the contractors are individuals, then it is no longer the 'people' as a corporate unit, or as a plurality of corporate units, that is conceived to bear an interest, or interests, or to have attached to it a right or rights; it is only individuals who are perceived as bearing such rights, only they who harbour interests which are accorded ultimacy and irrevocability. If we have a contract where groups are considered as bearers of rights, then the protection of their interests is ultimate; and where the interest of groups is ultimate, this must imply relative autonomy and self-containment *vis-à-vis* other groups within the society, including the state as the protective agency. Where individuals, however, come to be viewed as possessing ultimate rights, the rights of groups as such tend to disappear, for they can only be legitimated by reference to the more ultimate rights possessed by individuals.

Federal theory relates to both individual and group contracts, since both dictate a hard core of interest and of right (whether of the individual, church, province or otherwise) to be protected. The individual or the group yields a certain degree of autonomy in order to acquire a certain degree of protection; each concedes obedience to government in return for protection of certain rights and interests. Federalism is more intimately related to the earlier (the governmental) than to the later (the social) theory of contract in so far as it assumes that the basic, interest-bearing units within the federation are territorial (the states, cantons, provinces or whatever): the interest of these units usually being represented (as in the USA, Switzerland, Canada, Australia and elsewhere) in the upper chamber of a bicameral legislature. At the same time, federalism is more intimately related to the social than to the governmental contract in the degree that it assumes that individuals are the ultimate right- and interest-bearing units in so far as the direct operations of the federal (central) government are concerned. (This means that a federal government, while operating within its sphere, and even if it utilizes local or cantonal courts or administration, always conceives of those persons who are subject to its authority as constituting for such purposes its own citizenry and that it is owed a direct duty by them on that account, and not an indirect duty mediated by local or provincial legislatures.)

One can construe federal arrangements to mean that both individuals and groups have — within the federal polity — specific rights and interests, which it is the duty of this polity to protect. In contract theory generally, where private rights (of individuals or groups) are infringed, the duty of obedience — at some indeterminate point — ceases to be binding. The difficulty with federal (or any other) forms of government is that if the *individual* protests (an infringement of his civil rights, for example) he cannot effectively withstand the government *qua* individual, except, perhaps, by flight. The further difficulty specific to federal arrangements is that if the *group* (i.e. state or province) protests (an infringement of some aspect of its legitimate autonomy), it, too, is unlikely to be able to stand up to the central government, except, perhaps, by secession. But if it secedes, such secession makes it simultaneously impossible for federal citizens (i.e. those resident in the defector zone) to perform their specific duties of obedience to the central government.

A contract is commonly regarded as instituting some form of balance. But it may be regarded with equal justice as establishing an imbalance. Not all federations of course are based upon contracts, that is upon treaties. It is even arguable that none is. The West German government obviously is not. But even where we have the closest approximation to genuine federal contract — as in the case of the American union of 1789 — it still does not follow, in the strictest sense, that the contract creates a balance, even if we are entitled to say that it may reflect a balance. We might (with Wheare 1946) take the view that federal contractualism creates a balance, an equality, or *co-ordinate* authority between central and local governments. The idea that the centre operates autonomously within one jurisdiction and the locality within another implies, on a strict interpretation, that both centre and locality enjoy final say each within its separate sphere of control. This co-ordinate notion of balance is widely rejected today, for a variety of reasons. But the chief difficulty can be formulated as follows.

Federalism, whether centralist or decentralist, generally posits a coherent procedure which makes it possible to take final decisions within the system, while avoiding the theoretical extremes of both absolutism and anarchism. Federalism also presupposes a distinction between the centre and local governments. Either the local governments can generally be overruled within the system or they cannot be. If they can be, then they do not enjoy an autonomous power and their dependence demonstrates an imbalance. If they cannot be, this must mean that they can either take over the centre or simply secede from the federation. If a local government can take over, it is not equal but superior. There is a like difficulty, even if it only secedes. For within a federation, not only does the secession of a locality signify the cancellation of any federal authority over the territory; it equally signifies the cancellation of the central government's authority over its own citizenry within that locality. The effective secession of a locality therefore implies a net increase in the authority exercised by that locality, which again takes us beyond mere balance.

For a federation to have a coherent procedure which makes it possible for final decisions to be taken in any sphere, it must be possible somehow to amend any or all of its rules. Even therefore if one of these rules empowers a locality to act in some area without reference to the centre, it will normally hold that that rule can, none the less, be overruled — if this is strongly enough desired — without requiring the consent of the unit against which such action might be taken. Under the American constitution, for example, all amendments require ratification by 75 per cent of the states. But also under Article 5 of the constitution, 'no state, without its consent, shall be deprived of its equal suffrage in the Senate'. The effect of this article appears to be to leave to every state an inexpungible right of veto over any proposal to reduce its senatorial representation. In fact, however, and despite the practical political difficulties involved, it would be perfectly possible, legally, to amend article 5 by the simple expedient of deleting it — if 75 per cent of the states voted so to do. Contract therefore does not necessarily establish a balance; federal contract, more specifically, where it attempts to achieve a fully coherent constitutional order, necessarily in some sense excludes the idea.

The metaphor of balance is originally derived from a system of measures formerly current where the object was to determine the weight of an item, hitherto unspecified, by balancing it against another whose weight was already known. Within this system, the procedural norm to be adhered to was precisely and always that of achieving a 'balance' — since without this one could not establish the quantum of the unweighed item. If we remove ourselves from such a technical context, however, we cannot project as an ethical ideal the aim of achieving 'balance'. Where we adopt as a procedural norm the principle that every inclination, act or policy ought always or generally to be balanced or checked by the contrary inclination, act or policy, we are at once reduced to immobilism. Immobilism is the unwavering consequence of a quantitative principle of balance where applied to human decision and action. When we take any decision and engage upon a specific course of action, we move decisively beyond the metaphor of balance; we can even be said to display imbalance, disequilibrium, since the decision, the ensuing act, is firmly for itself, and not its opposite. Indeed, a perfect equilibrium between the forces supportive of unity, including federal unity, and those opposing it, must strictly imply the failure rather than success of any projected union. This is in no way to suggest that there is only one type of unity or one type of federation. It is only to say that where unity either objectively exists, or is politically desired, it will be at least as appropriate to speak of it as resulting from 'imbalance' as from 'balance'. Where the forces of national integration really are equally balanced against those supporting the continued independence of state units, the result can only be the failure of union.

A difficulty arises where 'federalism' is meant to convey a general or universal recommendation for balance, as where 'federation' is meant to convey an equally general or universal description of balance. Balance, taken in its physical dimension, is quite precise, conveying a quantitative notion of equilibrium or equality. But balance, taken as an ethical or ideological concept, although it frequently serves us as a convenient piece of shorthand, is, strictly speaking, inapposite. For that which is morally or politically right cannot be identified with or reduced to a state of balance or equivalence among sets of social forces. Were we to maintain that some given series of contestants were evenly matched — as perhaps Allied and Axis powers in 1942, or various independence movements and controlling colonial empires in, say, 1946, or non-racists and white supremacists in the American South in 1954 and after, or Tanzania's army and Amin's murderous rabble in 1976 — few of us would accept that these balances were practically desirable or ethically ideal, despite the relative equilibrium which such cases may display. In sum, any rapport between two social forces, although physically balanced, may prove morally repugnant. Equally, such a rapport may be quantitatively unbalanced, and yet prove morally desirable. Even the attempt to *describe* actual federations as balanced is subject to parallel strictures. Davis (1978) has drawn attention to the imprecise and misleading descriptive result which ensues when we seek to convey that a given federation is 'successful' by referring to it as balanced: for the 'balance' of forces from which it emerges not only may, but almost certainly must, be very much out of balance (cp. p. 139f). A true balance would dictate immobilism, not union.

It may often happen, of course, that some particular state of balance, of equilibrium, between rival social forces is ethically desirable. But this will presumably always follow from considerations independent of such balance itself. At any point where we intend that this balance of powers or of forces is desirable as such, *qua* balance, then we embrace anew the problem. For a mere quantitative balance of physical forces must often, morally speaking, simply fail to measure up. We conventionally maintain that 'might makes right' is a mistaken piece of ethics. The conclusion is not a highly contentious one. And in as far as that is so, there are presumably two immediate inferences which may be drawn from it. First, and more obviously, any given preponderance of might is not necessarily right. But secondly and less obviously, any balance or equilibrium of mights is not necessarily right either.

Federalism, as we have seen, may be reduced to a notion of balance, however inadequate such a notion may prove. The distinctive type of balance involved in federalism is, of course, territorial. 'Balance' itself is a much larger idea, as previously noted, and reveals no exclusive correlation with federalism: for this larger notion of balance could be considered with equal or greater propriety as an expression of constitutionalism. Yet it will not prove out of order to adumbrate here a vital aspect of the larger problem to which we must later return. The key argument for political balance in general, and not just for a federalist territorial balance, stems most directly from Montesquieu's formulae that 'power should place a limit on power' and that 'every man given power is apt to abuse it' (Book XI). The first thing to note is that these two formulae are quite different; in this connection we have already discussed the misleading way in which a quantitative notion of checking and balancing power is rendered equivalent to the moral notion of using it aright. Our present purpose is to direct attention solely to this immensely popular notion of power placing a limit on power. Calhoun (1851), for example, echoes Montesquieu's quantitative concern in almost exactly the same terms, except for the narrower, descriptive turn of phrase: 'only power checks power'. Acton, too, advances this Hobbist claim: 'power tends to expand indefinitely, and will transcend all barriers, abroad and at home, until met by superior forces' (in Himmelfarb 1952). It goes without saying that the notion of class struggle found in

Marx is at one with such an Actonian principle: political power is viewed as a by-product of control over the means of production; history is seen as a record of contestation between those who exercise such control and those who do not; hence the vital importance of revolutionary struggle and of 'the dictatorship of the proletariat'. Marx's argument, in effect, is also that 'only power checks power', except that he goes further to provide a view of what he takes to be the material and economic basis of power in society.

What we must now ask is what it is that actually happens when 'power checks power'. If we admit some form of objective existence for power, what we simultaneously admit is that it — its existence, its being — is not checked (in some sense). The existence of power implies the non-existence of a check (not *any* check) upon it. After all, power is merely a capacity to act. Such a capacity is only consistent with — which is to say that it requires — the absence or removal of such constraints (and checks so understood) as would convert this precise and particular capacity into an incapacity. Accordingly, to postulate any power implies a matching non-restraint, a lack of a check, upon the power we postulate. Yet this is in no way to imply that power as such has no limits. If we take it that power does not exist in the abstract, but is wielded by human agents, then no human agent, each being limited, can ever be held to exercise an unlimited power. Thus there is no inconsistency in maintaining, on the one hand, that no human agent ever wields an unlimited power and, on the other, that no bearer of power, in as far as he is a bearer of such power, can be subject to a matching check or restraint. We may also regard the notion that no human should be accorded total power (leave aside the question whether one can be) as consistent with the notion that accepting any political and social need for a power implies the acceptance of a matching need not to check or restrain it. (As when one says: 'Pick your man and let him get on with the job!') Power, as indicated, has limits, but these limits only demarcate the frontiers of powerlessness. What happens often enough, of course, is that a power accorded for one purpose is stretched to serve another, is construed too broadly, is improperly used, is abused, and so on. Restraints, safeguards and the like are vital for the containment of such developments. But it helps not to mistake or misconstrue their function: restraints in effect only insist upon a differentiation between powers that we think should, and powers we think should not, be exercised. Safeguards and the like merely insist that a power allocated for some specific purpose, and to be exercised in some specific way, should not serve any extraneous end nor invoke unacceptable methods.

A political system within which each power is precisely checked by another would not appear to be a feasible system at all. A political system in which each power of initiative is balanced against a matching counter-initiative, in which each social force is nicely blocked by some other, seems to represent a non-system, not a system — more an anarchy than a polity. A political system represents a whole within which the activities of individuals and groups are, up to a point, co-ordinated. Of course, there will be areas of activity which are not co-ordinated, and the basis of such non-co-ordination, as perhaps in regard to religious beliefs, may be consciously formulated as rights or be accepted as traditional practices. But the system *qua* system is less to be understood by what it overlooks than by how it coheres and by what it demands. And what often looks as though it is overlooked is in fact consciously omitted, but in such a way as itself to reflect a rule, the rule for example that, 'In this system, we neither interfere, nor permit to be interfered with, the individual's right to worship as he wills'. No system has a rule covering every contingency. Omissions may be inadvertant or deliberate. And where an omission is deliberate it implies a higher rule, that is that some principle of *laissez-faire* covers a stipulated area and is not to be infringed. A system is a vehicle for decision-making, both positive and negative, and the deliberate decision to omit to rule in a given province is only a negative decision, which in no way subtracts from the systematic character of the whole. A negative decision, such as that no official religion shall be imposed, may result from a balance of domestic forces, but it may equally result from a preponderant view within the system of such interference as intolerable. A system is characteristically systematic in as far as it reflects a preponderant sentiment, not just a balance of sentiment, whether positive or negative, for a given set of rules. In this sense, a system establishes a set of reasonably precise and coherent rules; these accommodate some types of behaviour and exclude others; these rules express an inclination, a preponderant weight; and this has less to do with equilibrium than with disequilibrium; less to do with balance than with imbalance.

A preponderant view or sentiment, as implied in any notion of system, may of course indirectly result from a balance of social forces — as intended by Figgis (1907) when arguing tolerance to be a residual legatee of religious quarrels, or by Watts (1966) when arguing that 'an approximate equilibrium between wider and narrower nationalism' is a prior condition for the construction of a successful federation. But a preponderant view never directly or necessarily emerges from such a balance of social forces. On the contrary, it happens that such a balance may prompt one of the parties to it to disrupt the equilibrium – which so often happens where civil war erupts. When by contrast the view is taken that the rule(s) associated with a given balance of social forces is (are) to be adopted as the preponderant view, this can only directly follow from the assumption that the acceptance of such rules is somehow regarded as preferable to alternative rules, taking account of the social costs which would attend establishing these.

We begin to approach the suggestion that the formula '*only* power checks power' is acutely misleading. Power does check power. But it is not only power which does so. Indeed, when we have reached the state where only power itself can achieve the effect, then the position will prove both unusual and parlous. This generally inapposite notion of power checking power can only cover extreme and aberrant cases. There are of course such cases. And there is nothing wrong or untoward about casting our minds beyond the usual to contemplate the worst that may supervene. But even when we have done that, some truth remains in the aphorism that hard cases make bad law. One cannot properly equate an individual's value with the very worst behaviour of which s/he is capable. Neither can one maintain that power is *only* checked by what is no more than one of the available means of restraining it. Naturally enough, one may so extend the meaning of power *qua* check as to equate it with any effective restraint whatever – such as the 'power' of a song to soothe a petulant child, or the overpowering reasonableness of a petitioner which earns the admiration and support of authority. We need not complain about usage. But if we permit the extension we must insist upon a distinction. For we may intend by power only force, the big battalions, an army, the policeman, and so on. Or we may intend this plus any other capacity that generates an incapacity – such as indecision, disagreement, shame, self-restraint, respect for oneself, respect for others, respect for truth, for fairness, and various forms of toleration. In any event, we should be clear. The significant consideration is that power *qua* force or compulsion is not the typical nor the most important sort of restraint which we place upon power – whether understood in the narrower or broader sense.

If we read 'power' as 'force', we may see that it everywhere affords some support to government but is nowhere a viable means of government. To paraphrase the wisdom of Dean Inge: 'one can do everything with bayonets except sit on them'. Power may best counter the power of the crazed rifleman firing from the clock tower or of the governor who seeks physically to debar minority children from entering a local school; for there is always some occasion on which it is well to fight fire with fire. But fire is often better fought with water. And one important means of containing violence is by not repaying it. If Mungo Park, at the close of the eighteenth century, had tried to fight his way through West Africa, he would never have returned from his first expedition. David Livingstone, by contrast with Henry Stanley, got about reasonably easily in East Africa, basically on his own, relying very little upon bullets and bayonets. The wily Odysseus, by guile, made his way safely home. Many are the models to which we could advert. The resort to a narrow sense of power to contain power may be necessary, but it is not typical or representative. An army or police force may be needed as a reserve, but beyond a shallow threshold the more force is used, the less effective it becomes in rallying support. Indeed, the potential power (*qua* force) available to a government is probably greatest precisely where its survival least depends on it. Governments then are not only, nor mainly, run by checking power with power, and most especially where 'power' in both cases is read in a narrow sense.

To conceive of government as a mere mathematical balance, one generated and controlled by variegated group inputs, is all very well, but, overall, is highly implausible. If a government is a government, if it represents a discrete system of control, then it impliedly contains some preponderance of power. A true equilibrium is an immobilism, is the absence of a governing power. A preponderance of power may, naturally, take on the appearance of a balance – as in a coalition where the parties comprising it are of equal strength. But the government *qua* government consists of the preponderant agreement among those parties that they should constitute and run the system as they do. What counts is the effective thrust of the arrangement, not the fact that the parties agreeing it may be equal or nearly so – their equivalent strengths may as often lead to feuding and war as to mutual accommodation. No government can or may do whatever it wishes, but the fact that the power of government is limited is still perfectly consistent with the notion that a government is to be understood as wielding a preponderant power.

The formula, 'only power checks power', does not then capture the reality. But, to be fair, that is not its exclusive purpose. As a descriptive statement, it is mistaken. The mistake is readily overlooked since the purpose in making it is moral. If it is *only* power that does or can check power, then it is impliedly useless our seeking to secure restraint through argument, persuasion or other such means. When we do not wish to consider these other possible means of restraint, then we can rule them out with the sort of restrictive formula adduced. What that formula implies descriptively, but mistakenly, is that a person or group, being objectively or somehow quantitatively less powerful than another, can never hope to induce the latter — except by force, threats or similar measures — to yield or relent on any significant point of difference between them. If all of this were so, it could only be foolish to recommend the contrary. Where we really assume that power is simply 'bound' to expand, it is merely inconsistent to tax it with a failing which we initially insist it cannot avoid. Kant's observation still holds: ought implies can. And any feat that cannot be executed ought never to be demanded. And any feat inevitably executed ought not to be complained about. Hence we confront the moral burden of the principle, 'only power checks power'. This moral may be roughly stated as follows: 'No power that requires to be checked ought ever to be pleaded with or even complained about but merely confronted and contained by an equal power'. But it will not be difficult to see that such a call can only lead into either immobilism or some form of war — in short, back to anarchy. If we establish a system, then we establish a preponderant power; no matter how much we divide and balance that power, in as far as the system is systemic, it must retain — its rules must describe — some sort of preponderant thrust; that preponderant power or thrust is, as such, unchecked; for we cannot simultaneously concede it and block it; but we can stipulate what that thrust should be, as distinct from what it should not be; and although this is not strictly speaking to balance power, it does demarcate its outer limits; and it is only in such demarcation that we confront the initial and essential character of any constitutionalism worth the name.

An *a priori* doctrine of political balance, like the *a priori* doctrine of political decentralization, ends up in the swamp of anarchism. In any true balance, it will be clear that the forces involved are in equilibrium, and that none enjoys any advantage — which may translate out as authority — over any other. It is an anarchical situation that obtains where all central power is so diffused among the components of the system that none is anywhere left that may be devolved. Federalism, conceived as anything other than a 'weak' ideology of balance, is not very satisfactory. As an ideology of balance, whether ideologically 'weak' or 'strong', it is certainly not distinctive. Centralist and decentralist federalisms are inescapably territorial doctrines, whether calling respectively for a more or less powerful centre. But federalism, where conceived as a doctrine of balance, is neither more nor less centralist, and because of this, it need not necessarily be expressed in territorial terms at all. Federalism as balance has accordingly more to do with constitutionalism in general than with territoriality in particular. Federalism presupposes constitutionalism, but the acceptance of constitutionalism, as in France, Sweden, Norway and elsewhere, does not necessarily imply support for specifically federal institutions. For the moment, we may say that constitutionalism is more broadly to do with a polyarchic (i.e. a multi-centred or plural) system of control, while federalism — excepting the 'balanced' variety — may be characterized as that species of constitutionalism more restrictively concerned to secure that the components of this polyarchic system, in at least some significant respect, should be specifically regional or territorial units, irrespective of the type or degree of centralization or decentralization achieved within the polyarchic limits of the system. Accordingly, the more general discussion of federalism as balance can be seen as a most appropriate preliminary to the discussion of constitutionalism as such.

PART TWO

FEDERATION AS INSTITUTION

I do here walk before thee like a sow
That hath overwhelmed all her litter but one.

(Henry IV)

6 ANALYSIS, NORMS AND FACTS

Method of Definition

Contemporary observers appear disinclined to provide definitions of federation (e.g. Duchacek 1970; Sawer 1976; Davis 1978). The basic reason for this aversion stems from the fact that governments called federations have materialized in such an overwhelming variety of forms that any stipulation which covers every one of them appears to run the risk of encompassing virtually any kind of government at all. Consider the range of states which are commonly said to be federations (leaving aside those which have ceased to exist). In North America, there is Canada, the USA and Mexico. In South America: Brazil, Argentina and Venezuela. In Europe: West Germany, Switzerland, Austria, Czechoslovakia, Yugoslavia and the USSR. In Africa: Nigeria, Sudan and Tanzania. In Asia and Oceana: India, Malaysia and Australia. Where one seeks a common tie between all such governments, whether to do with superficial constitutional form or with substantive behavioural practice (whatever the form), one will not come away with a very great deal.

Despite the difficulties, we continue to speak and write about federations. In doing this, we assume that they share certain common characteristics. We assume that they are marked by some common logic, without which they cannot constitute a genuinely distinct class of governments. Unless we speak and write so loosely as not to wish to convey anything at all, then we are bound to stipulate − however broadly, even provisionally − what that logic is. Such stipulation is not required in any discussion where a common understanding already exists regarding the terms in use. It is to be regretted that such an understanding no longer obtains in discussions of 'federation'.

The variety of meanings associated with federation creates a genuine basis for misunderstanding. We must recognize, however, that this is not a situation which it is possible ever entirely to avoid. When we indicate, in the end, what we take a federation (or any other noun) to represent, we must accept from the outset that the exercise is in some degree arbitrary. Before anything of a more substantive sort is said about federations, it will help to delineate the contours of the conjoint arbitrariness and rationality involved in definitions.

Consider that, in indicating what a federation is, we may advert to the range of examples which it denotes, such as the cases cited above. If we begin with denotation, then we arbitrarily identify the states which we hold to be federations, without revealing why we consider them so. This beginning — the naming of cases — is arbitrary. It closes off the range of instances to be included. But given this initial closure, we may subsequently embark upon a quite different, indeed an empirical, rational process, involving us in the business of identifying such features as exist commonly between and exclusively for the states we originally denominate as federations. In denotation, then, stipulative arbitrariness is involved in the cases first marshalled; empirical investigation becomes operative only from that point in the attempt to establish any exclusive behavioural constants as between these cases.

Alternatively, we may eschew examples of federation and begin by stipulating the principle which we assume the idea of federation to connote. If we begin thus with connotation, then we formulate the distinctive characteristics of such states as we shall identify as federations, without providing examples of these. This beginning — the stipulation of a distinctive criterion or of criteria — is also arbitrary. It closes off the range and type of behaviour which any system, where adjudged a federation, can be permitted to display. But given this initial closure, we may again embark upon an open empirical process — here with a view to determining which actual systems satisfy the abstract federal criteria originally advanced. In connotation, therefore, stipulative arbitrariness is involved in the governing criteria first formulated; empirical investigation becomes operative only from that point in the attempt to locate which systems of government meet these criteria.

In practice, analyses of this sort begin either denotatively or connotatively. But, logically, the beginning is always implicitly connotative. We may not be able consciously to express our reasons for considering a given range of countries to be federations, but without some implicit principle binding them, they cannot be taken to represent a coherent assemblage of examples. If, moreover, we cannot elicit that principle, we cannot explain the sense in which these examples are federations; we cannot explain what it is that the examples exemplify. To escape the difficulty, we may well talk more loosely about federations exhibiting family resemblances. This would be to suggest that federations are not differentiated from other systems by any one or more exclusive criteria; and that some federations share some characteristics, that others share other characteristics, while all are conceived as linked in some looser, chain-like fashion. As against this consideration we need only note that families are not identified by a cluster of physical appearances (phenotype) but by simple biological descent (genotype). Thus, contrary to much popular sentiment, 'family resemblances' (often only imagined) are strictly subsidiary to the precise and exclusive criterion of descent from some stipulated set of progenitors.

The conclusion that we come to is that the analysis of any phenomenon, like federation, must always imply some explicit or implicit connotative stipulation regarding what it is we intend. This stipulation, when explicit, is a definition; when implicit, an assumption. In practice, of course, the student caught in the two-fisted grip of examples and criteria cannot but squirm. There is a reasonable procedure, however, to which one may resort in seeking an escape.

(1) One can inspect a limited number of those states which most observers agree to be federations.

(2) One can identify the range of basic, and apparently exclusive, features which they share in common.

(3) Converting these features into formal criteria, one can apply them to all other states to see which of the latter fit these criteria.

(4) One can either decrease the criteria to expand the range of cases, or increase the criteria to contract the range of cases. There appears to be an intuitive advantage in decreasing rather than increasing the criteria to be employed. (The more numerous and complex the criteria designating an area of study, the more difficult analysis becomes, and only in part because there are fewer cases available for empirical study. We can so define federation that it will only fit the American or Canadian or Australian case, for example, and no others. To the extent that we do this, to that extent do we also diminish the prospects of any comparative political analysis.)

(5) On the assumption that we decrease the criteria, it is to be assumed that we should try to do so only in such a manner as to accommodate the bulk of those systems conventionally regarded as federations.

(6) Our criteria should not only allow us to identify federations, but equally systems that are not federations, which means that the criteria involved must not merely stipulate what federations are presumed to hold in common, but must stipulate only those common features which are *exclusive* to federations.

(7) We may accept that possibly some few of those systems traditionally designated federations shall no longer — on the criteria stipulated — be so designated; equally, that some systems not conventionally called 'federal' may qualify under the stipulation provided.

Federalism and Federation

It is essential to begin by distinguishing between federalism and federation. Federalism is here construed as some form of doctrine – even a variety of these. Alexandre Marc (1961) agrees that federalism 'became a doctrine' (p. 14) in the nineteenth century and that P.-J. Proudhon was the greatest of these doctrinaires. Proudhon (1863) wrote that 'truth is one', that 'Truth' led, politically, towards a single doctrine and constitution, and he concluded that 'the sole constitution which an astringent reason will compel the peoples of the world to adopt is federalism' (p. 20). Marc sees federalism as becoming 'this revolutionary awakening [*prise de conscience*] which today provides the essential condition for our salvation' (p. 117). Marc's practical concern was to promote a federally united Europe. His federalism was of a 'balanced' type, committed to promoting 'diversity in unity'. But his wider view is similar to Proudhon's. He believes it appropriate to understand federalism in 'the widest sense' – which is to say as a 'fundamental commitment which renews and transforms all commitments' (p. 16). He views federalism as marked by a 'mystical' capacity to restore faith in our fellows, to engender 'new and constructive solutions' by embracing 'all of man's activities, problems and preoccupations'. Partial solutions, Marc declares, are inadequate and he urges upon us the view that federalism is 'une doctrine totale'. Despite this comprehensiveness of outlook, Marc is quick to maintain that federalism is not totalitarian. Marc even denies the 'ideological' character of such federalism as he espouses. All that he means, really, is that federalism is not oppressive, closed, unarguable. For the rest, Marc and many who think like him promote federalism as a coherent and inclusive view of the world – at once philosophical, legal, anthropological, sociological, economic and political, a doctrine supposedly providing a sound basis for not only understanding but also directing the affairs of the world. This sort of comprehensive federalism, whatever contrary claims Marc may make, is most certainly ideological. But whether comprehensively and clumsily ideological, or more openly philosophical, such federalism is to be distinguished from federation, understood as a more limited institutional arrangement, a device indeed which has not and cannot resolve that whole range of problems which scholars like Marc might wish to end through its agency.

Federalism, taken philosophically or ideologically rather than institutionally, most frequently appeals for a marked degree of regional independence and autonomy. So understood it has close affinities to European liberalism and political pluralism (cp. Follett 1918). Such pluralism generally describes and (more relevantly) recommends varieties of decentralism — whether (in historical order) within a government (as in versions of the balance-of-powers theory) or between the different regions of a system (as in territorially decentralized federations) or between the different classes/ethnic groups/associations at work in society (as in the functional articulation of overlapping interests sometimes appealed to in the theory of cross-cutting cleavages or cross-cutting pressures). Pluralism reflects a much broader theoretical concern than federalism. But federalism can still be fitted within it. The commonest way of doing this, as suggested, has involved identifying federalism with decentralism, but most especially with territorial decentralism. All the same, decentralism has by no means proved the sole orientation of federalism, given that federalism assumes several distinct forms. Federal theories have not only recommended decentralism, but also centralism, as well as doctrines of balance — and theories of balance may, of course, as easily reflect a centripetal as a centrifugal orientation.

Any existent form of federation can be consistent with any one of at least three types of federalism. A federation can be established in order to secure greater centralization, or with a view to greater decentralization, or to achieve some form of balance. Since all of these ends, where posited simultaneously, are mutually inconsistent, it will not help us, where we seek to understand federation in reality and as a whole, to try to reduce its actual, empirical character to any one of these three philosophical or ideological orientations. This is not to say that a federation will not betray some moral or normative orientation. All human institutions, and most especially political institutions, must do so. But the normative orientation will change over time within each federation and will vary as between them all. We shall identify the constant and exclusive recurrence of significance within federation as the entrenchment of regional or territorial representation at the national centre.

We shall take it that federalism is some one or several varieties of political philosophy or ideology, and that federation is some type of political institution. The intention is not that such a distinction is widely observed, but only that it is useful. Nor is it intended that philosophies/ideologies, on the one hand, and institutions, on the other, are entirely different, since it appears reasonable to assume that institutions are often either sprung from philosophies/ideologies, or do in some vaguer sense reflect them. We need not here concern ourselves greatly with the distinction between political philosophy and political ideology. A political philosophy may be broadly taken to refer to any open, reasoned and coherent political analysis which somehow penetrates below the surface of things (this last understood as day-to-day policy). A political ideology may signify any extended description and analysis of the world which also seeks to provide it with guidance and direction (concatenated recommendation) of a closed, circular and unarguable kind. There is a degree of argument opposing such a philosophy/ideology distinction (e.g. Seliger 1976) and some supporting it (e.g. King 1968 and 1977).

It will suffice for present purposes to say that an institution is only a complex of practices, that practices are rule-governed, that all rules recommend forms of behaviour, and that all recommendations are on occasion (and indiscriminately) labelled 'ideological' or 'philosophical'. All institutions, then, implicitly recommend forms of behaviour. Every federation, taken as an institution, has some recommendatory component or character. And if we equate recommendation with philosophy or ideology, then every federation has a philosophical or ideological character. Although a philosophy or ideology will not necessarily take on an institutional form, any coherent set of institutions may be regarded as giving expression to some set of philosophical or ideological postulates. Although there may be federalism without federation, there can be no federation without some matching variety of federalism. It is not the names 'federalism' and 'federation' that matter, but the distinction we here use them to underscore. Accordingly, to expand on what was first said, 'federalism' will advert to some political principle or ideal, taken on its own, while 'federation' will betray a predominant concern with an institutional set of facts — in the form of basic, recurrent interactions. It is obvious that these interactions, which we summarily refer to as institutions, could not persist — did not a reasonably numerous body of people continually regard the endurance of such behaviours (for whatever reasons) as somehow and on balance appropriate or desirable. Federalism and federation, we conclude, are distinct. But some form of federalism is always implicit in any given federation at any given time. This federalism, however, that we shall espy in every actual federation will not readily equate with any of the conventional federalist philosophies of decentralism, balance, or centralism. The 'federalism' in federation will involve nothing more than the promotion of that degree of support for local territorial units sufficient to enable the latter to serve with and as a part of the central or federal government on some entrenched basis.

Empirical Investigation

We can only proceed to empirical investigation of federation from the point that we entertain or accept some convention regarding its nature. Basically we propose that any federation be regarded as an institutional arrangement, taking the form of a sovereign state, and distinguished from other such states solely by the fact that its central government incorporates regional units into its decision procedure on some constitutionally entrenched basis. The object of most of the subsequent discussion in this book is indeed largely directed towards justifying such a convention. Whether or not this discussion is adjudged satisfactory, it is clear that some convention must be advanced as a necessary condition for any more strictly comparative, empirical research into the nature of federation.

It is not difficult to demonstrate the importance of the conventions we choose to adopt. Suppose we were to define federation in a manner different from that which we have chosen — perhaps in terms of (a) an institution created by contract which (b) concedes a degree of local autonomy and which (c) establishes a central government possessed of both military and diplomatic powers. Given such a definition (it might well, of course, be mistaken for a simple factual observation) one might then proceed to hypothesize that federations allow greater regional diversity than do 'unitary' states. In following up such an hypothesis, however, one might slap upon it a negative conclusion. This unanticipated outcome might flow from such an observation-statement as that 'Australia, a federal state, reflects no more regional diversity than New Zealand, a unitary state'. Parallel observation-statements might be advanced for the United States *vis-à-vis* the United Kingdom; Malaysia *vis-à-vis* Indonesia; Nigeria *vis-à-vis* Ghana; Yugoslavia *vis-à-vis* Poland etc. (We have omitted any convention regarding the meaning to be assigned to 'unitary state' — except that it implicitly hints at a 'non-federation' — but this omission does not greatly matter for our present purpose.) Having accepted such observation-statements as these, we might seek to explain the failure of our hypothesis on the grounds either that (a) federations are not the *only* states which reconcile some local autonomy with some central direction, or (more strongly) that (b) *all states*, including federations, marry some local autonomy with some central direction.

It is not difficult to detect what has gone wrong in a case of the sort instanced, where we advance a convention regarding the subject we are to investigate, advance hypotheses relating to the actual behaviour of the subject under investigation, and turn up unexpected results. The basic fault often, as here, lies no further afield than the convention with which we began. If we initially stipulate federations to be distinctively federal by virtue of combining local autonomy with central control; and then conclude that federations allow no greater degree of regional autonomy or decentralization than some or all other states; and this on the grounds that some or all other states in effect have the same features we initially assigned to federations; then all we have demonstrated is that the definition we advanced for federation is not distinctive, that it is too broad, that we have not established a proper analytical distinction between federations, on the one hand, and those states, on the other, with which we seek to compare them empirically. The surprise contained in the 'empirical' result would merely follow from the logical ineptness present at the beginning — in the unrefined and imprecise character of the chief analytical stipulation first advanced.

To make empirical comparisons between human organizations — social, economic, political or other — one cannot ignore or omit stipulations or conventions which draw a determinate line between the institutions to be compared. Otherwise, there is no objective basis for comparison, which is to say that we cannot know that the phenomena we seek to compare are in fact either distinct or similar. The setting out of precise and mutually exclusive conventions about meaning is to the social sciences (including law) what axioms are to algebra. However we define the character of federation, the chief danger to avoid is that of giving too broad a stipulation. If we are quite precise about what we mean by federation, then it should be easier to determine whether any given aspect of its actual performance is to be regarded as peculiar to federations only, or characteristic of all states in general.

If we define a federation as a state which combines a degree of local autonomy and central direction, then, as we have seen, there is nothing in this to distinguish it from any other state. If we add to this definition the rider that federations must originate from contract, this may provide the distinctiveness required. A problem will arise, however, when we are asked to determine whether this 'contract' may equally be written or unwritten, as also to determine the minimal conditions it involves. Thomas Hobbes's explanation for the origin of *all* government was, for example, basically contractual. He contended that when a people submit to a sovereign from fear of him, they do so up to a point by their own choice and so contractually; and that when they agree among themselves to form a union, they also do this contractually, but from fear of one another. The problem is clear. If we seek to distinguish federations from all other states by reference to their supposed contractual origins, we shall require to be quite explicit about the range of meaning we include in 'contract'. The reason is implicit in the powerful case presented by

Hobbes: any union, and any government so understood, must in some degree repose upon the voluntary assent of those it governs. Accordingly, any state, federal or otherwise, unless we stipulatively guard against this, can be conceived as based upon a 'contract'.

Whatever we might stipulate federation to mean, let us consider an hypothesis about actual performance, here regarding the conditions out of which federations may be thought to emerge. Hypothesize, then, that federation originates from 'fear' or in response to 'threats'. The analytical problem directly posed is that the notions of 'fear' and 'threat' may be interpreted, and operationalized, in highly variable ways. If we do not indicate at the outset what eventualities we intend these key expressions to exclude, then our conclusions may be of an overlapping — which is to say confusing — sort. A threat to one state from another may be held to stem from their pursuit of different objectives, whether cultural, political, economic, military or other. Alternatively, 'threat' may merely be equated with the overt expression of an animosity irrespective of the underlying balance/imbalance in military-economic strength between the states involved. By contrast, 'threat' may be read into some act of political, economic or military mobilization. A threat may even be read into a condition of weakness on the part of one state which creates the possibility of its being overrun or manipulated by another in a manner detrimental to the interests of a third. It may mean the clear likelihood of imminent attack. There are many additional possibilities which we need not set out here. The point yet again is clear. The meaning of 'fear' or 'threat' can be understood in a variety of ways, so much so that any state can be held to regard any other, however powerful or powerless, as a 'threat', thus arguing for union with it or against it and in either case on grounds of self-defence.

We must at all costs avoid quibbling over words. But if meanings are unclear and overlapping and indistinct, then our inattention must block any prospect of grasping the reality, whatever we may suppose this to be. Consider now more substantively the view that federations originate from fear. Take three rather distinct types of case.

First, an assembly of independent states may believe themselves subject to some common, external threat and, instead of each of them attempting an individual defence, they may coalesce into a federation (Riker 1975). This circumstance held in some degree, for example, for Switzerland and the USA. Secondly, a federation may not only be created from fear of those who remain outside it, and against whom it is formed, but equally from fear by some prospective members of other prospective members. This circumstance held in some measure for Nigeria and Malaysia (Birch 1966). Third, every federation may be held to originate from an actual or potential threat, whether of an internal or external kind.

In each of these cases, a basic question to be cleared up is whether what is said is meant to apply to federations alone, to other states as well, or to all states whatever. From the literature involved, no clear conclusion can be drawn. It is also to be noted that, in as far as 'threat' is given no precise and restricted operational content, we shall never experience any difficulty in discovering the presence of a 'threat', both external and internal, not only at the origins of federations, but equally in the founding of non-federations.

The chief point about the first and second positions noted above is that they either cancel each other out — or lead one into the third position. To begin, whether we say that federations are formed from fear of non-members or from fear of associates, it is clear that we refer initially to the *origins* of union. If it is true (a) that some federations arose (at least partly) from fear of prospective non-members, and equally true (b) that other federations arose from fear (at least in part) of prospective members, then clearly neither (a) nor (b) can be exclusively true in the sense that either provides a valid explanation of the origins of *all* federations. If we then move on to the more comprehensive contention that all federations originate from either external or domestic threats, there may be no great difficulty involved in conceding this to be true — but there will be no great difficulty either, barring further analytical refinement, in showing it to be trivial. If the more comprehensive notion is valid, it must be so for all unions, not just for federations, and will therefore in no way constitute a distinctive attribute of the latter. There is, presumably, no political community for whose founding one can ever entirely confirm the absence of security motives (cp. similar conclusions in Voyenne 1976: 39 and Davis 1978: 133). The only way in which we could conceivably push beyond this conclusion is by beginning with a more precise analysis of 'security motives'.

Let us assume that every state system, federal or not, has some defence capability, both domestic and foreign. Let us further assume that this capacity has, as its correlate, some fear or apprehension that the system may be challenged in some non-peaceful way, either from abroad or at home. In as far as these assumptions hold valid for all systems, they must equally hold for all federations. In as far as these assumptions hold universally, then the fearfulness, the threat, which is asserted to hang over every federation, cannot be regarded as a distinctive characteristic of federations. This then would be a good reason — in the context of the present analysis where we seek to determine what distinguishes federations from other systems — for jettisoning the hypothesis that all federations distinctively and significantly originate in or persist from the presence of foreign or domestic threats.

Imagine an observer, concerned 'scientifically' with predicting how federations will behave, to assert that a necessary (if not sufficient) condition for federation coming into being (and presumably persisting) is the presence of some threat. One might accordingly explain the collapse of the West Indian and Central African federations, for example, by reference to the absence of such a threat. We have already observed, however, that the evidence can always be so construed as to reveal a threat. In the case of the West Indies, it could have been the 'Yankee dollar' or 'British imperialism' etc. In the case of the Central African federation, the threat could have been (and was) African nationalism or Soviet interference or South African expansionism or Western imperialism. To say in this way what the threat could have been is no more than to say that these were *de facto* perceptions of threat discernible (i.e. held by some agents) within the system. None the less, these federations failed. Of course, they were originally imposed in some degree (by the British Colonial Office). But then West German and Canadian and Australian and other federations were also in some degree originally imposed. There was in all these and other cases some perceived threat. Yet some federations fail and others survive. If one seeks to predict which federations will succeed and which will fail, and assumes that the perception of a threat will guarantee success, then no federation should ever fail.

We may wish to shift the discussion to another level, by attempting to stipulate what degree of threat must obtain before it becomes likely that a federation will succeed. But no one has shifted the discussion to that level. Even if someone did, however, the going would not be easy. The USA originally perceived a serious threat from Europe and achieved a stronger union. Canada has perceived as a serious threat Quebec's secession, and has responded with a looser union (similarly with Sudan and Tanzania). Pakistan perceived a serious threat of Bangladeshi secessionism, but the upshot, despite armed intervention by the centre, was the end of the union altogether. In short, it is nothing like self-evident that, as the seriousness of a threat increases, the prospect of a successfully united federation in every case swells accordingly.

It is understandable that some observers should believe, where any state enters into a union, that it only does so because it is somehow 'compelled'. There can indeed be no question that all federations do begin under some form of compulsion. It may only be, however, where federal ventures are entered into or put up with, that it is for 'compelling reasons' not always of a military kind. Henri Brugmans (1969), as a proponent of European federation, takes the view for example that 'if a federal Europe is to come into being . . . it will not be born of a civil war . . . nor from an external threat [such as the USSR] nor be imposed by a hegemonic power' — such as France, Germany, Britain or the USA (p. 127). Brugmans and those who think like him may or may not be proved correct. What is clear is that no extant analysis would legitimate the conclusion that what he writes in this regard is demonstrably foolish.

One may argue that federations arise in order 'to meet an external military or diplomatic threat or to prepare for military or diplomatic aggression and aggrandizement' and that '(1) the expansion condition and (2) the military condition' involved in this 'are *always* present in the federal bargain and that each one is a necessary condition for the creation' of a federal state. Here the concept of 'threat' is simultaneously identified with self-defence, on the one hand, and with territorial aggrandizement, on the other. This is alternatively put in terms of the prospective units of a federation desiring 'protection from an external threat or [desiring] to participate in the potential aggression of the federation' (cp. Riker 1964: 11–12). The position is put later on (Riker 1969: 139) in terms of federation originating 'in a plan of local governments to retain autonomy when creating a central government for defense or expansionist purposes'.

Riker's exposition is, in general, of the highest quality. It remains that the argument we are now inspecting is unsatisfactory. First, if federal governments are formed from 'local governments' — which, if not independent, are at least not dependent upon one another — then there initially exists no overarching government nor any 'federal' politicians of whose purposes one need take account. The decision-making units, on this model, are only the 'local governments' themselves. Now the objectives of these units may be formulated in terms of (1a) mutual cohesion in response to threat *or* (1b) mutual cohesion in pursuit of expansion; or in terms of (2a) mutual cohesion in response to threat *and* (2b) mutual cohesion in pursuit of expansion. What one cannot do is to formulate the objectives of these units simultaneously in terms of (1) *and* (2). But this is what happens where we are told that the expansion condition *and* the military condition 'are *always* present' and simultaneously that the concern of the local units is to secure protection against external threat *or* to expand by participation in potential aggression.

In other words, the central case made to date for a strict correlation between the emergence of federations and the presence of a threat to local units is simply unclear (even self-contradictory) in what it maintains. This consideration becomes important where one attempts to explain the failure of any federation. If federations minimally require condition (2) to succeed — that is a conjunction of external threats to local units *plus* an impulse on the part of these units to expand — then one shall explain failures, at least in part, by reference to the absence of *both* these conditions. If, by contrast, federations minimally require condition (1) to succeed — that is an external threat *or* an impulse to expand — then we shall *not* explain failures by reference to the absence of the two conditions together. There is to be remarked, of course, a notable difference between the idea of 'threat' where it means that a collectivity is being *threatened*, and where it means that a collectivity is itself *threatening*. Do federations arise (a) because local units are threatened; or (b) because they themselves threaten (others and promise themselves) expansion; or (c) because these factors are merged at the appropriate time? Riker's hypothesis has not been sufficiently refined to provide an answer. It variably suggests that the absence of (a) or (b) or (c) will explain failure.

One may of course explain the origin and consequently the failure of federal union in other terms than the threat of attack or promise of territorial expansion. It is as well to note, however, before we inspect other alternatives, that 'threat of external attack' is not a part of the meaning of federation (where conceived as a contractual arrangement between independent entities). The idea of 'territorial expansion', by contrast, is a part of the meaning of federation where the latter is defined as a freely contractual 'bargain' between otherwise sovereign entities. Thus it is empirically conceivable, on a contractual definition of federation, that federations could coalesce from the emplacement of a 'threat', but, on the same definition, the prospect of 'expansion' is already assumed, or logically presupposed. If it is definitionally assumed (as by Riker) that a federation is a contractual arrangement between otherwise independent entities, then it must follow that this assumption cannot simultaneously be treated as an object of empirical investigation. The definition, containing this expansionist assumption, draws a circle round what is to be investigated *in other respects*. We cannot, then, in effect define federation as an expanded political union, contractually grounded, and then proceed to declare that we have discovered that this concern for expansion is the — or one of the — empirical *causes* of federal union.

The comprehensive explanation of the origins of federal union as a function of fear may reflect the influence of Hobbes (as in Birch 1966 and Riker 1975). We remarked earlier that Hobbes explains all unions in these terms: either a people are conquered, and submit from fear of the conqueror; or they form a compact, in order to avoid the brutish and fearsome inconvenience of unregulated interaction with their fellows outside the compact. 'In both cases', he says, 'they do it for fear' (*Leviathan*, II, 20). If one speaks, instead, of a 'threat' rather than a 'fear' being at the origin of all federations, nothing much is changed. One is entitled to make a broad case for a threat or fear being present at the foundation of any union. To press what is, in effect, the same argument for federal unions will not pull us clear from the edge of the trivial, unless we at least refine terms like 'fear' and 'threat' both by type and degree. Otherwise, to claim the presence of a threat is perfectly compatible with other claims for the universal presence of contrary conditions: such as hope for a better future, for peace, for economic gain and so on. For all of these, in some equally broad sense, are probably equally present at the founding of any union.

Moving beyond the question whether or not some element of threat is present at the founding of federations — there is always some circumstance, internal or external, that may be so construed — we next approach the question whether this threat or fear, which some will always perceive, is universally to be accorded a higher explanatory value than all other factors. If we take West Germany as an example, it may be claimed that it was formed from fear primarily of Soviet communism, or from fear of domestic Nazism, or from fear of the Western Allies who in fact both occupied and governed the country. One can make a case for each of these options. None the less, it was perfectly clear by 1947 that there was no question of America surrendering additional German territory to the Soviets, nor of pro-Nazi parties being allowed anywhere to form on German soil, nor of the West pursuing a scorched-earth policy in those areas subject to its control. These considerations do not, of course, exclude the presence of German fear. What they do underscore is the historical inconvenience of according to 'fear' any higher priority (in the founding of the *Bundesrepublik*) than, say, to German 'resignation' or German 'hopefulness'. Many West German officials, for example, 'hoped' to proceed with post-war reconstruction with Western aid within the political limits imposed by the then *de facto* rulers of West Germany. Many, if not most, equally 'hoped' to be able to rejoin East Germany, even if at some highly remote point in future time.

There is a difference between federation conceived as an ongoing contractual arrangement and federation conceived as originating from fear. These positions can none the less be merged — as in Hobbes's analysis. The upshot is a conjoint contention that all federations are contractual and that such contracts originate from fear. If one contends that all unions originate from fear (or threats), one does not, as indicated, specify the relative importance of threats as over against, for example, hope, greed, fatigue, etc. One may contend, on the other hand, that all unions (including federations) originate from voluntary contract. For even when states merge under threat, in a sense they still do so voluntarily, in as far as they remain able to ignore the threat, if at a cost. But we may recognize here, too, as in the first case, that such a contention does not in itself in any way establish the relative importance of freedom as over against compulsion in such a 'contract'. It is for this reason that one is entitled to ignore contract theories, not only as applied to the origin of federations, but as applied to the origin of any form of union whatever (cp. King 1967: ch. 7). A theory of contract so large, that it encompasses as 'voluntary' assent obtained by whatever means, up to and including threats and actual force, cannot prove very helpful. But we shall return to 'contract' in the following chapter.

T.M. Franck (1968) gives every appearance of presenting an alternative view to that of 'threat' as 'the' indispensable condition for federal union. His position clearly seems to be that what is necessary for successful federation is the presence of 'a . . . positive ideological commitment to the *primary* goal of federation *as an end in itself*'. He argues that where this primary ideological commitment is lacking, failure (as in East Africa, Central Africa, the West Indies and Malaysia) becomes probable (p. 173). Franck suggests that federation can meet such needs as territorial expansion, achieving larger markets, containing social conflicts, securing military defence and so on, but 'only if the political leaders have first themselves embraced federalism as a social good in itself, and have persuaded the populace to accept an ideology of union not — or not merely — because of the shortrun benefits in money or power' (p. 182).

Riker (1969) seeks to bolster his own view — that federations which fail are those without 'apparent need either of defense or of conquest by means of a stronger central government' (p. 139) — with the support of Franck. This is understandable in view of the fact that Franck (1968) prefatorially salutes Riker's argument as 'effective' (p. xiv). Riker, however, contends that Franck 'identifies' or equates his primary ideological commitment to federation itself with the presence of 'a common enemy'. The identification, alas, appears to be Riker's, not Franck's. Franck does remark that the 'presence of a threatening common enemy' as also of 'a vision of almost limitless conquests and wealth' can significantly contribute to consolidating a primary and positive commitment to federation as an end in itself, taking the USA, Canada and Australia as examples (Franck: 186–7). But nowhere does he equate such a 'secondary factor' with what he calls 'the primary factor' of commitment to union as an end for itself. In fact, Franck (p. 172) quite firmly assigns 'security against attack' to the position of a 'secondary' cause (or goal) of successful federation.

What we have seen then is that different views may be expressed, on the empirical level, regarding the cause of the formation of federal unions. What we have also implied is the importance of distinguishing between definitions of federation and subsequent hypotheses about other aspects of their operations. What is interesting in the case of Franck's argument — to the effect that federations require a primary commitment to union *per se* — is that it is not really empirical but definitional. He accepts Friedrich's formula which stipulates a federation to be 'a union of groups' with common purposes and distinct identities — without (understandably) being impressed by it. None the less, it is clear that one cannot picture a union as a union without regarding its members as being committed in some sense to it. This commitment must be a part of what we *mean* by a union: conscious engagement as opposed to mechanical interaction. Empirical inquiry, accordingly, cannot be greatly helped where we end by demonstrating what is already implied in our definitional point of departure. It is all very well for Franck to imagine that 'a single, highly structured definition of federalism' is not needed (p. 169). But the lack of reflection on this point in his essay suggests a contrary conclusion.

In sum, any empirical hypothesis about federations (or any other social phenomena) must first clear certain crucial analytical hurdles. There is, of course, to begin, the problem of specifying quite plainly, coherently, and exclusively the meaning to be attached to 'federation'. Moving beyond this stage, an empirical hypothesis, say, about the *emergence* of federations, may posit an explanation in terms of the presence of an initial 'fear' or 'threat' serving as a necessary if not sufficient condition for their formation. There are further analytical hurdles such an hypothesis must clear. First, the range of conditions meant to be covered by 'threat' must be precisely and narrowly drawn, in order to make sure that some phenomena are excluded and also to help to identify such phenomena. If this is not done, we merely guarantee in advance that the conditions we 'hypothesize' to be necessary shall always prove to be discoverable in some form at the origins of all unions. Secondly, we must establish the priority of importance we accord to the conditions we stipulate to be necessary *vis-à-vis* other conditions which we hold to be more necessary or less so. If this is not done, then it is always possible, after the fact, to maintain circularly that the importance of the threat we actually discover is equal to that which we anticipated as necessary in relation to other conditions present, whether or not the latter were stipulated.

7 DEMOCRACY QUALIFIED

General

Federations are non-absolutist, which means that they are in some degree democratic, although if we used the expression 'constitutional' instead, we might inspire less confusion. Federations are to be understood as democratic only in the sense that they involve some form of corporate self-rule, of a kind where it is constituent territorial units which comprise (at least some of) the agents involved in this process of rule. It is important to exclude any idea of federation as democratic where our formulation takes us beyond the minimalist position already set out.

First, the voting populations of the different territorial units in federations are always of unequal size, sometimes dramatically so. Since the votes of citizens in some territories will have greater force than those of citizens in other states, federations must in this sense, and in varying degree from case to case, prove undemocratic.

Secondly, all that is minimally guaranteed in all federations, we shall suggest, is the entrenched position of constitutive territorial units, not the rights of individual citizens. In this connection it is to be observed that Australia, Canada (up to 1982) and India, for example, either have no bills of rights at all or have bills that are qualified in such a way, formally, as to allow governments to uphold them or not, depending upon their assessment of the public interest at the time. In these countries the weight of informed opinion has often opposed the principle of unequivocal entrenchment of rights, commonly for fear that too great authority would be conferred upon judges. The federation of the United Arab Emirates, it has been observed, 'is definitely feudal rather than democratic' (Hicks 1978). In the hundred years and more that followed the 1848 consolidation of the Swiss Union, the vote was denied to women on both cantonal and federal levels. In 1860, one-third of the population of the American South consisted of Blacks, only a fraction of whom (251,000) were styled as 'free coloured'.

Third, even the constitutive territorial units of federations do not in all cases genuinely 'agree' to either enter or remain in the union. The consolidation of the Swiss Union in 1848 was based exclusively upon the military defeat of the Catholic (Sonderbund) cantons by Protestant cantons in 1847. The survival of the American Union in 1864 was again built upon the military defeat of the Southern by the Northern states. It was not altogether willingly that 555 princely states were frogmarched into the Indian Union in 1948. Germany embarked upon post-war federation under Allied pressure.

For all of these reasons, it is clear that one cannot unqualifiedly characterize federations as 'democratic'. They are only so across the board in a strictly limited sense. Ursula Hicks (1978) is correct, up to a point, where she writes: 'The objective of federation is a form of government for the people by the people. That is to say it is *inherently* democratic' (p. 4, my italics). The only problem is that this sort of statement may be taken to imply considerably more than the evidence will allow. In summary, although federations are constitutional, and in this sense democratic, they are not *per se* fully democratic.

Equality of Representation

Federation is to be regarded primarily as an institutional arrangement, as opposed to an ideological perspective. Under this arrangement, distinct national and regional units of government are assigned somewhat distinct powers within a perhaps new sovereign whole. At least some of the powers of the regions are entrenched, not by virtue of rendering the regions sovereign, but by constitutionally incorporating them into the decision-making procedure of the federal centre. Simultaneously, all citizens of the various regions are rendered directly subject through equal citizenship to the authority of that centre. Due to the incorporation of the regions into the national decision-making structure, as also to the conferment of fully national citizenship upon the peoples of the regions, the citizenry of each region enjoy some degree of direct control over the central government, while the central government is equally engaged in some degree of direct responsibility towards the people as a whole. The net effect of this situation is that an entitlement to secession cannot coherently or consistently be conferred upon the regions. A parliamentary system, by contrast, whose members (or deputies or congressmen) represent nationwide interest- or professional groups only, to the exclusion of entrenched territorial units, is in such degree more aptly to be styled a 'corporatist state' than a 'federation'.

Governments of every political colour have resorted to federation. Witness the union between Zanzibar and Tanganyika, on the one hand, or the accommodation between northern and southern Sudan, on the other. It does not matter that these are not *called* federations. The truth is that a new union in each case has been established such that the major territorial units involved have been accorded an entrenched form of representation at the centre. There are observers who are *a priori* opposed to federation because they perceive it as a source of national weakness. (This was the case with Kwame Nkrumah when advocating African unity.) And were federation introduced into such states as the Netherlands or Jamaica or Mauritius it would almost certainly prove cumbersome. On the other hand, there are observers who *a priori* favour federation because they assume that it must necessarily produce liberty, tolerance and compromise (e.g. W.A. Lewis 1965). But where federation was introduced into the West Indies (1958) and in Nigeria (1954) it most certainly had no such effect. The point is not that federation works differently in different countries; this is both obvious and unavoidable. The relevant point is that the only residue with which we are left is the constitutional entrenchment of constituitive territorial units. Federation, so conceived, is no more appropriately to be regarded as the object of blinkered hostility than of blind adoration.

While it is largely true that 'no government has ever been called federal that has ever been organized on any but the territorial basis', it has been argued by some that the emphasis upon federation as a legal relationship between distinct territorial governments exercising different powers is not only inadequate but irrelevant to 'the essential nature of federalism' (Livingston in Meekison 1971: 21-4). This position is argued basically on the grounds that one cannot understand the institutional character of federation in any given setting unless or until one understands the underlying social conditions which generate these institutions. Livingston's point is that federations emerge in circumstances where social diversities are sufficiently strong to require to be recognized, but not so strong as to inhibit integration — producing in consequence a compromise between national integration and the retention of local autonomy. This is almost certainly true, even if it does not tell us a great deal. Beyond this, however, to say that we can only determine whether a system is genuinely federal by examining the society in which it is located, must none the less presume that we attach some coherent meaning to the expressions 'federal' and 'federation'. It is no use insisting that federation 'is not an absolute but a relative term'. If it is to be used meaningfully, it has to be given some reliable and fairly fixed sense. It is clear that federations differ markedly one from another. But if we cannot say in what minimal sense they are alike, neither can we reliably pinpoint the myriad differences between them.

Any federation, in as far as it is a self-governing corporate unit and of a type which accords a distinctive position to its constitutive territorial units, is to be viewed as non-absolutist, as constitutional, in this sense as a democracy, but of a polyarchic* rather than a mono-archic* kind. A mono-archic democracy may be understood as the most complete type of democracy one might achieve, in the sense that its constitutive, right-bearing units are its individual citizens alone, all formally equal. By contrast, a polyarchic democracy, as in any federation, is perforce incomplete because it not only embraces individual citizens, with an equal entitlement to the vote, but also individual territories or states or provinces, which also enjoy some form of equal influence at the federal centre. This equality between territories, as a practical matter, must always in some degree subvert any strict equality between citizens. This is so for the reason that representation by geographical region (possibly by *size* of region) and representation by size of population within a region are two distinct principles: they cannot be counted upon to coincide. We may illustrate this by reference to an American case in point.

In the United States, each of 50 territories (states) enjoys formally equal representation in the powerful upper house (Senate). But — the most extreme example — tiny Rhode Island (sometimes referred to as a 'rotten borough') is entitled to the same representation in the Senate as is California, despite the fact that California has a population twenty times larger than Rhode Island's. On these figures it is clear that the proportionate power of the average citizen of Rhode Island in the US Senate grossly exceeds (by 20:1) that of the average citizen of California. To repeat, the entrenched representation of the territorial units of a federation on a roughly equal basis (these units as a practical matter having almost inevitably unequal populations) is such that federal democracy is universally incomplete. In saying this we must leave to one side consideration of the situation in non-federal democracies.

Separation of Powers

Any assumption of a necessary connection between contract theory and a separation-of-powers theory would be misplaced. In the case of a

---

*The sense of these terms is more fully developed in a forthcoming book on *Constitutionalism* in this Series.

contract, it is assumed that each party surrenders a good or service to some other on promise of some benefit. The problem with a contract is to secure enforcement in case of default — hence the need for a third party (perhaps the shaman, the government, the law, the state) to perform in this capacity. The separation-of-powers technique stems from the consideration that the third party required in a contracting situation may somehow prove a party to such disputes as arise. It is where the government is considered unequal to the task of remaining above the battle that the separation-of-powers theory comes into its own. It is precisely where it is assumed that the contractual model is unworkable — that there is in general no 'indifferent' judge to adjudicate social disputes — that observers pitch upon the notion of restraining those in power by reducing or dividing such power as is allowed them. The contractual approach accordingly (which merely sets up an arbiter) is one thing and the separation-of-powers approach (which seeks to control the structure of the arbitral procedure) is something else again.

Absolutism has most commonly been associated with monarchy and aristocracy. The most conventional assumption is and has been that these are overturned by achieving democracy. Absolutism has been identified as a circumstance in which one or some control(s) others without their consent. Democracy has been identified as government by the consent of the governed. Thus, once it comes to be assumed that democracies, too, can be absolutist, one encounters a difficulty. In what sense can a government which governs with the consent of the governed be absolutist? And even if an absolutist democracy were possible, how could those consenting to it be defended against it? To come to the conclusion that even democratic power is absolute, is to conclude (on one moral reading of the matter) that all power is evil. The accompanying assumption is that it must be either diminished or destroyed. And perhaps the only way of doing this is by breaking it up — hence the separation of powers.

The characterization of democracy as an absolutism springs from the theory of sovereignty, where Hobbes, most significantly, is concerned to argue that any sovereign, including a democratic one, must prove as absolute as any other (cp. King 1974: ch. 18). Rousseau, though his formulation of the problem was a dramatic one, did not write without precedent when he maintained, in effect, that democracy (appearances to the contrary) can be established without prejudice to those claims for absolute, unlimited, indivisible and perpetual power thought necessary in every sovereign state. What was not and has not been properly appreciated, is that any form of corporate sovereignty — whether called aristocratic or democratic, but as distinct from such sovereign power as is wielded by an individual – is somehow necessarily divided. Corporate sovereignty, if ever it is to work, requires a set of rules which impose upon the 'sovereign' its sovereign character. These rules provide the necessary ground for a democratic sovereign's existence, and by virtue of this make such a sovereign at all times subject to some rules which it cannot be understood to stand above (cp. King 1974: 244–50).

All of this will suggest that a federation, taken as some type of corporately sovereign system, could not – were it absolute – be sovereign. To say that there is a *corporate* sovereign implies that no single individual is dominant; that the units incorporated are in some degree equal, which means limited; that there are regularized exchanges (often meetings) among or between them; that there exist decision-procedures to which all members are subject; that there is some acceptance or guarantee of freely voiced views, etc. There is always a division of power within any group which functions as a corporate unit in the sense that no total or absolute right of decision is concentrated upon any one individual member. But there is no division of power where and if this is taken to mean that the decision-procedure for such a corporate unit is incoherent. One rule, for example, may be that enactment of a decision requires a majority vote. Though members may be divided in both their views and votes, there is no incoherence attaching to the decision-procedure for so long as there are no seriously conflicting rules, as for example to the effect that the same category of decisions must be carried equally by majority and by unanimity.

A federation, then, taken as a corporate body, can automatically be regarded as featuring various divisions of power, while simultaneously being regarded as a coherent and, in this sense, single, sovereign entity. But the unity and coherence here attributed to federations can just as readily be attributed to all other sovereign corporate bodies, whether we call them 'unitary' or anything else. The thrust of this position, accordingly, is that if we wish to maintain that federations, in some general sense, are *distinctly* characterized by some division of power, we are mistaken. Every sovereign that is genuinely corporate can be characterized in precisely the same way – whether it be unicameral or bicameral or tri-cameral or even quadri-cameral (as the Swedish Parliament once was and as the French Fifth Republic in a modified degree remains) or federal or otherwise.

Bicameralism

We may now consider the notion that every federation has as its 'exclusive hallmark . . . the presence of an explicit "division" of legislative power in the constitution' (Davis 1978: 142). The same point has been made more dramatically thus: 'In federal states no choice [between unicameral and bicameral systems] is open because [federations] are *by definition* two-tier in structure' (Amellier 1966: 3, my emphasis). In arguing that a division or separation of power is the exclusive hallmark of federations, one may intend at least two different things. The first is that only federations are characterized by such a division. The second is that all federations have this characteristic, whether or not non-federal systems do so as well.

If we take it that only federations instance a separation of legislative powers, the assumption is mistaken. A great variety of non-federal states do and have featured legislatures divided into two or more bodies. The Swedish, Dutch, British and French Parliaments, for example, represent only a few of those many states which are not normally regarded as federal but which are none the less bicameral or multi-cameral. The point is not that federations display no legislative division of power. They display, on the contrary, a great deal of it. The relevant consideration is that this display alone in no way distinguishes a federation from a non-federation.

If we take it that all federations instance a separation of legislative powers, this assumption, too, is mistaken. It is of course true that most federations have first and second chambers in their legislatures, and that the second chambers — as in the USA, Switzerland, Canada and Australia — are generally and basically structured with a view to representing the interests of the component territorial units. But three considerations weigh against the possibility of our saying very much more. First, federation in Cameroon and Pakistan did not in fact lead to bicameralism. It still has not done so in Yugoslavia. We have noted above Amellier's asseveration that federal states have 'by definition' bicameral legislatures. Fortunately, the author is prepared to permit fact to contradict 'definition'. The counter-examples cited, he allows, 'show that a bicameral system is not an inescapable element in the structure of a federal state' (Amellier 1966: 7). Secondly, although federal second chambers may have the constitutional power to influence legislation, this power, as in the case of Canada's appointive second chamber (senate), may prove essentially a paper power. Third, a second chamber — apart from not existing in every federation, and apart from sometimes proving quite unequal to the task of effectively defending states' rights even where it does exist — is simply not to be regarded as everywhere and necessarily indispensable to the accomplishment of such a defence.

Consider that the division of the central legislature of a federation into two bodies — the second of these representing the constituent territorial units — is merely a device intended to secure that the regions always enjoy distinct and effective representation *qua* regions at the federal centre. Precisely the same end may be achieved within uni-cameral legislatures by different means. Perhaps the simplest means, where a second chamber now exists, would be for the procedures presently used to elect (or select) the members of this chamber to con-tinue. Once the procedure determining the membership of the second chamber is fixed, then rather than form a second chamber, the member-ship (i.e. its voting units) might simply be added to those voting units already present in the first chamber.

Suppose, for example, members of a second chamber to be popu-larly elected (as in the USA); such elections might continue, with the difference that those elected (to represent the states or regions) would be assigned as members of the first (and now sole) chamber. Suppose, by contrast, members of the second chamber to be appointed (as in Canada); here again they could be assigned to the first chamber. (This is a move which would in practice be resisted because it would give such appointees considerably more power than they presently exercise — although their numbers could be reduced to compensate for this.) If the actual members of the second chamber were elected by and from the first chamber, those so elected could merely be assigned an additional or supplementary vote — within the single and only chamber. The point is not that unicameralism is abstractly preferable to bicameralism or to multicameralism. The point is merely that it would appear perfectly possible, with only a minimum of tinkering, to change every existing bicameral federation into a unicameral one without in any way weaken-ing the entrenched representation of the member states at the centre. (In some cases, perhaps in most, the effect on the contrary would be to strengthen — as would occur in Canada — the entrenchment of the component territorial units.) For all of these reasons, therefore, it is inappropriate to regard a bicameral legislature as a distinct and essential characteristic of federations. What is distinctive is the entrenchment of regional representation.

8   CONTRACTING OUT

An Original Contract

Bernard Voyenne (1976) among others insists upon federation as a *foedus* (derived from *fides*, implying an agreement that is freely and mutually consented to). Hence his conclusion that 'no federation can exist unless there is a deep commitment, entirely devoid of both reservations and compulsion' (p. 27). S.R. Davis (1978), in seeking out a common element between federations, similarly finds nothing except '*foedus*', or covenant. 'The idea of covenant betokens not merely a solemn pledge between two or more people to keep faith with each other, to honor an agreement', he contends, but it also 'implies the recognition of entities' on the assumption that there can be no covenant without mutual recognition – in short, 'no reciprocity between an entity and a non-entity' (p. 3). P.-J. Proudhon (1863) is the most notable of nineteenth-century figures to view contract as a universal and necessary characteristic of federal union.

There are senses in which it is correct to say that federations instance contractual relations. The component territories of a federation may, for example, have entered the union by their own free decision. Alternatively, these component territories, however they entered the union, may require genuinely to negotiate with the federal centre over various matters (in some cases the distribution of tax receipts, or the development of natural resources, or the location and control of national parks, etc.). For these and similar reasons, accordingly, we might refer to federations as contractual. This sense of 'contract', however, is very broad and may reduce to little more than 'agreement'. Where we say that federations are contractual, but only mean that they are based upon some level or degree of agreement, it will be clear that we say nothing that is distinctively characteristic of federations, since it is perfectly legitimate to maintain that any union, whether federal or not, must involve some agreement among its component units: not everything can be done with bayonets.

Thus, the characterization of federation as contractual may prove trivial – certainly in those cases where contract is broadly equated with agreement. We may, with a view to avoiding this trivialization, restrict the range of application of the notion of contract *qua* agreement – as where we refer, first, to the *origins* of a federation and, secondly, to its *ongoing legal and behavioural properties*.

Let us address the question of origins. The USA (1789) and the German Confederation (1871), for example, came into being by virtue of agreement among independent entities. Such cases illustrate the manner in which federations may be based upon contract *qua* agreement in the sense that it is by this means that they may first have emerged. The case for the contractual *origins* of federations, as illustrated by examples of this kind, is not trivial. For the contrast between voluntary and compulsory entry is quite clear — even if somewhat less so in the German (1871) than in the American (1789) case. It must be noted, however, that the tenable case to be made is only that *some* federations originate contractually, not that all do. And if a contractual origin for federation is not universal, then neither can it be necessary.

All federations do not originate from contract. We have already mentioned the Swiss case (1848) where the incorporation of the Sonderbund cantons was based upon their military defeat in 1847. If we take a Southern perspective and regard the American Union as having been dissolved from 1860, then the 1864 re-incorporation of that region was also essentially military. Similarly, India's princely states were not presented with a free choice regarding their integration in 1948. In the Soviet Union and in Yugoslavia, the federal regime did not emerge from below by free agreement among independent entities, but was inspired and even imposed by the centre. In Nigeria, the dissolution of the three large 1952 provincial units (Northern, Eastern and Western) into 12 and then (1976) into 19 smaller states was carried out by military governments following the 1970 close of the Biafran War. But perhaps the most singular, recent case in point is that provided by contemporary West Germany.

At the conclusion of World War II, Germany, for all practical purposes, was broken in two by her Western and Eastern conquerors. The part that was to become the Bundesrepublik (West Germany) had its component territorial units restructured: eight of today's eleven West German *Länder* (or provinces) were not traditional but were unilaterally devised by the Allies. In April 1945, the United States Joint Chiefs of Staff moved towards 'the formation of a central German government with carefully defined and limited powers and functions' (Directive 1067). This process culminated in the Bonn Constitution of 1949. This constitution, though it governs the functioning of today's Bundesrepublik, was less freely agreed to originally than accepted under duress by the West Germans. As Sawer (1976) correctly observes, 'there is a widespread dislike for the federal system in West Germany, probably fed to some extent by a feeling that the system was dictated by the American and French conquerors' (p. 105). Had the Germans been able to act more independently, they might well not have adopted a federal system at all. Neighbouring Austria, for example, although federal, has a much tighter constitutional structure than Germany, with only the faintest entrenchment of regional power. East Germany (the GDR) as of 1968 abandoned its 1949 federal constitution. This is not to suggest that confederal and federal experience were in any way alien to Germany — her history from 1815 through 1933 clearly demonstrates the contrary (cp. Pflanze 1963 and Hamerow 1958). Indeed, without this backdrop, it is difficult to imagine an imposed federal structure working so well. What we are entitled to say is that the historical direction of German commitment was away from confederation to federation, and beyond federation to the removal of entrenched powers for component regions. West Germany's present constitution was not, and apparently was not intended to be, ratified by a popular vote. Certainly, the Parliamentary Council which agreed the constitution was never elected. The West German leadership was no doubt opposed to securing popular confirmation of what they expressly conceived as only a provisional constitution. And it was provisional for them largely because it left the two Germanies divided. But it was provisional, too, because its basic features were imposed — including this separation of West from East.

The Bonn constitution was designed less to keep Germany 'whole in the face of conquest' as maintained by Riker (1975) than to ensure that it should not become too powerful following recovery from defeat, as maintained by Dikshit (1971). Willy Brandt, former German Chancellor, tells the story that American Secretary of State Dulles insisted to him that the one point on which the US and USSR were agreed was that Germany should remain divided (BBC telecast, 18 Oct., 1979). More directly, the Commander-in-Chief of the American zone in Germany, General Lucius Clay (1950), *à propos* of the new German constitutional arrangements, recorded that the French and American governments were 'interested in principles which would avoid the creation of powerful central control'. According to Clay, the German 'constituent assembly' — it was later agreed that such an assembly should be called the Parliamentary Council — was to be instructed by the occupying powers to 'draft a democratic constitution' of 'federal type' to protect the rights and freedoms both of individual citizens and of the member states of the new union. Clay put it on record, too, that only the occupying powers would, in the end, determine whether or not the proposed

'constituent assembly' met these conditions (pp. 398-400). The proposed constituent assembly was re-styled the Parliamentary Council
basically due to the recognition that there was no popular support in
Germany for the sort of decentralized constitutional formula which this
assembly was expected to disgorge. For the same reason, the new West
German constitution was not called a constitution or *Verfassung*, but
the 'Basic Law' or *Grundgesetz*, this last providing for its own displace-
ment in its final article at such time as 'a constitution adopted by a free
decision of the German people comes into force'. Quite apart from
Clay's account, the Allied Military Governors' Aide Memoire for the
Parliamentary Council, dated 22 November 1948, is on record as stipulating that the new *Grundgesetz* would only be accepted if it provided,
among other things, for a bicameral legislature (with entrenchment of
state or *Land* representation in one of the houses), a limited executive
subject to legislative or to judicial review, a limited legislature checked
by 'an independent judiciary to review federal legislation', and the exclusion from federal control of 'education, culture and religious affairs'.
(The Aide Memoire is reprinted in Golay 1958: 263-4.)

As J.F. Golay has observed, the French, British and American governments all 'opposed a strong central government' in Germany. Basically,
the Allied position 'favored a division of powers between the constituent
Länder and the central government' with all residual powers – those
not expressly delegated to the central government – reverting to the
Länder. The chief difficulty derived from French opposition to 'any
power of taxation' or control over police being conferred upon the new
federal centre (Golay 1958: 5-9). The Allied stance was perfectly
understandable – given the unparalleled excesses of Nazi rule. But the
widespread German reaction to the Allied stance was equally understandable. This reaction was at first negative for the reason, as Carlo
Schmid, the Social Democrat, correctly observed, that the *Grundgesetz*
effectively represented an imposed arrangement which appeared to confirm the separation of the two Germanies. It was only after the stark
choice of 20 July 1948 was presented to the new local government
authorities (the German ministers-president of the *Länder*) that they
must either accept the Allied framework or prejudice hopes of Marshall
Plan assistance – together with the prospect of German recovery which
this carried – that official German opposition swiftly and sensibly col-
lapsed.

The ministers-president on 25 July 1948 appointed a committee to
draft proposals for the new *Grundgesetz*. This committee met on 10
August 1948 at Herrenchiemsee and as early as 23 August yielded up

a complete and detailed draft to be submitted to the German Parliamentary Council. The proposals subsequently agreed by the latter were in part rejected, on review, by the Allied powers. The Parliamentary Council further amended these proposals until agreement was reached with the military governors in May 1949. If the federal *Grundgesetz* was devised, as Riker maintains, principally in order to forestall a Soviet threat, it is perhaps significant that, in its initial form, it made no provision whatever for national defence.

The involuntary element usually involved in new unions is rarely broached. But it will not help to overlook its presence. One observer offers the following comment.

In the case of constitutional systems conceived . . . in a period of Western military occupation, acceptance on the part of the Western powers of a certain 'democratization' of the defeated Axis powers could normally be expected to be a condition precedent to Western acquiescence in the return of sovereignty and self-government. It is, perhaps, hardly surprising that both judicial review of the constitution and also [federation] in the case of West Germany, and judicial review in the case of Japan, should figure so prominently in . . . these particular countries. Judicial review and [federation] are considered by very many American lawyers as [essential to] constitutionalism . . .

The writer concludes that 'American opinion, whether actively applied in direct political pressure or not, was quite decisive in the "reception" of these particular . . . checks and balances' both in Germany and Japan. (McWhinney 1966: 129. Riker objects to this characterization of the West German constitution. Brugmans 1969: 18 endorses it.)

What is clear, however, from the preceding account, is that American and Allied pressure was direct. One may well wonder why so elementary a fact should be disputed at all — especially in light of Allied insistence upon Germany's unconditional surrender, which could scarcely serve any useful purpose if not conceived with a view to restructuring Germany's post-war system. Indeed, all countries which become independent or regain independence under the aegis of another power — as with the many federations which achieved independence under British imperial tutelage — are likely to inherit a domestic political system produced in some degree by external dictation.

In the German case, we are confronted with a decentralist concern, one less peculiar to the Germans themselves than to those who effectively controlled a vanquished German state — or at least part of it.

Whether German opinion will come to accept the *Grundgesetz* as a *Verfassung* lies with the future. But the object of the Allies – effectively in power from 1945 – was, for perfectly limited and practical reasons, to create a weaker state than that with which they had battled ruinously twice within a century. The chief device in achieving this object was a decentralist federalism. For any people to be able to employ a constitution, they must, in at least some loose sense, be regarded as 'accepting' or 'agreeing' it. And so with West Germany *vis-à-vis* the *Grundgesetz*: thus far may we travel the road of contractualism. But if the intention is that the German *Länder* of the post-1945 period were traditional, that their representatives were elected, and that these freely and without duress agreed among themselves to form a federation, then we confront a significant historical distortion. We are entitled to regard the Bundesrepublik, in its essentials, as an imposed arrangement. We need not, however, by reason of that imposition, regard it as non-federal: it works, as it has done, for over three decades, and it betrays a significant entrenchment of regional power. Accordingly, the contention that federations are universally and necessarily of a freely contractual nature, where we mean that they all originate by free agreement among sovereign entities, must appear less than convincing.

Even where a federation does originate from contract, it is as well to identify the latter's strictly limited and unilateral character. Normally, the most important relations for a member state or province are with the federal centre, not with the other states or provinces. But precisely at that point where genuine contracting parties may be hypothesized to exist, that is immediately prior to union, that party which normally becomes most powerful in federal arrangements, that is the central government, does not exist; and a contract in which the most powerful party takes no part must appear somewhat odd.

The new centre created by a federal union lies at the heart of the matter. The federal centre is not merely an arbiter: it is itself a government. It has its own independent power, which it draws from constituent regions and from the citizenry as a whole. Where this new centre is voluntarily created, the original parties agreeing to it only succeed by surrendering some part of their power. The distinctive identities of any original contracting units are blurred such that 'they' no longer survive in the manner that may have characterized them prior to union. The original contract, if between sovereign equals, may well leave them equal, but not sovereign, and thus not as they were. After union, a centre which did not previously exist now exists. The legal identity of states which were perhaps formerly sovereign is transformed.

The new loyalty owed by the citizens of local units to the federal centre after union is not legally revocable by these (modified) units acting unilaterally, nor by the citizen acting individually. The federal centre moreover does not effectively envisage its own dissolution and, for this reason, is legally and often practically irreversible. A structural inter-dependence between centre and periphery which could not, heretofore, have obtained, now obtains. A legally uninhibited entitlement to compose or brawl with other units can no longer be freely engaged in law. The right of any unit to withdraw has been implicitly foresworn (see ch. 9). In sum, in as far as any state enters into a federation contract-ually, this state, after union, is not in law the same, nor exercises the same rights and powers, as before.

A Continuing Contract

We may now focus upon that notion of federation as 'contractual' where the intention is to locate the character of present, ongoing legal relations. In this context, 'contract' may refer to a continuing agreement between two or more parties. There will be two important elements in such a contract: (a) the terms or substance of what is agreed, and (b) possible provisions for enforcement of these terms.

As for *terms* . . . These, in any agreement, are subject to variable and divergent interpretation. Accordingly, there will be three possible pro-cedures, satisfactory or not, to determine what the agreed terms are.

a_1 Authoritative interpretation of a contract may lie exclusively with all of the parties to it. If these interpretations are not in accord, it only follows that nothing has really been contracted, at least as far as the substance of these divergences is concerned. This implies that the terms are only such as are or come to be unanimously agreed. Here it is assumed that the substance of any valid under-taking is plain and that the consequential obligation upon con-tractants to execute is firm (*pacta sunt servanda*).

a_2 Authoritative interpretation of a contract may lie with only one or some of the parties to it. Thus, given an agreement between X and Y, then X (perhaps father or employer or bishop) may assume or be accorded the right, in case of disagreement or misunder-standing, to decide what was agreed, or how what was agreed is most reliably to be applied. If, however, one of the parties to a contract wields this sort of exclusive right to interpret and apply its terms, such a contractant can be under no obligation to view as valid any interpretations save his own. The interpretive equality of standing projected under a_1 and a_3 is lost under a_2.

a_3 Authoritative interpretation of a contract, finally, may lie with an external agent, an independent arbiter — 'external' or 'independent' in the sense of not being one of the contractants (as in the case of the International Court of Justice; or, for some purposes, Britain's Privy Council; and generally as with any arbitrator who is agreed upon by two disputants without being accorded an authority to compel).

As for *enforcement* . . . We must assume, to begin, that the terms of the contract are clear — as they must be, by implication, where provision is made for some authoritative interpretation of what they require, allow or exclude. Given as much, 'enforcement' will merely comport such action as may be taken to compel a contractant to meet obligations incurred or to provide compensation where there is a failure to execute. There are three possible procedures governing enforcement.

b_1 Enforcement may remain the preserve of each party to the contract. If, however, all contractants have authority to interpret the contract (as under a_1), such that what *was* agreed can only effectively reduce to what is *now* agreed, it is difficult to conceive that any occasion for enforcement, as defined under b_1, can arise. For no party to the contract need interpret the latter in any way that places an obligation upon self which this party is unwilling to execute.

b_2 Enforcement may become the preserve of only one or some parties to the contract. Thus, in any agreement between X and Y, not only may X (as under a_2) serve as authoritative interpreter of the contract, but may wield, in addition, an exclusive executive or police power to compel execution or exact reparation. If, however, a contracting agent wields an exclusive power of enforcement of this kind *vis-à-vis* other contractants, it is difficult to imagine how this agent could compel self to comply, and therefore ever be subject to enforcement at all. The equality of standing between contractants *vis-à-vis* enforcement, as projected under b_1 and b_3, is lost under b_2.

b_3 Enforcement may lie with an independent arbiter, 'independent' in the sense of not being one of the contractants, and 'arbiter' in the more substantive sense of wielding a compulsory power.

A contract, then, taken as an ongoing legal relationship, will normally and in its fullest sense contain or assume provisions for the authoritative interpretation and enforcement of its terms. As shown, there may be three distinct provisions each (a_1 through b_3) for interpretation and enforcement. None of these provisions applies comfortably to federations.

Having regard to a_1, federations do not leave authoritative interpretation of their constitutions to each member territory. Having regard to a_2, there may be serious doubt whether this arrangement is best viewed as 'contractual' at all; and in any case, even, if we do choose to view it as such, the conclusion must be that all states, not just federations, are contractual. As for a_3, no federation, if fully sovereign, leaves authoritative interpretation of its own constitution to any external agent. Having regard to b_1, no federation allows each member unit to enforce the federal constitution by the independent power of decision of each such unit. As for b_2, the same remarks apply as for a_2. Finally, regarding b_3, no federation, if fully sovereign, accepts the entitlement of any external power to enforce constitutional arrangements internal to the federation.

It will be helpful to elaborate upon the summary position set out above, first taking a_3 and b_3 together. In the case of fully sovereign federations, there exists no agent external to (or independent of) the arrangement, enjoying an authority to interpret or to enforce its terms. There was no provision, when for example the USA and Switzerland first came into being, for any external or independent power to either adjudicate or police the arrangement. Moreover, where there is such an agent (perhaps a colonial or occupying power) it surrenders its power of enforcement (as did Britain in India and Malaya) at precisely that point where the federation comes into being as an independent (or fully sovereign) entity. Where an opinion is invited by a federal government, as from a Privy Council or an alien Parliament, the assumption must be either that what is sought is an opinion only (not a binding decision in the sense that the external author of it is entitled to enforce it) or that the author of the request is not fully sovereign. In any event, if we restrict attention to cases like those of India, Switzerland and the USA, the formation of the union in each case conferred sovereignty upon the federal centre, which was so structured as to entrench representation of constituent territorial units.

One might argue, in the Canadian case, at least up to 1982, that the ongoing character of the federation was contractual because of the right reserved by Westminster independently to control amendment of the Canadian 'constitution'. But here, the form of independence conceded by the United Kingdom under the terms of the British North America Act of 1867 was simply incomplete. Any fundamental amendment to that Act remained the preserve of the British Parliament. For as long as this situation persisted, Westminster could be viewed as performing an arbitral function — not between Canada's various provinces — but between the federal centre, on the one hand, and the provincial periphery, on the other. Under the BNA Act, the provinces were granted major control over civil rights and property, while the federal centre was granted major control over trade, commerce, money and banking, together with all unnamed residual powers. This could be construed as a form of balance — whether broadly between centre and periphery, or more narrowly between English and French language groups — with Britain retaining a reserve power to thwart any basic amendment to the 1867 arrangement. To the extent that Britain retained such a reserve power, Canada would have to be regarded as only partially sovereign.

Only a few points need be made. First, if Canada (prior to 'patriation') is to be held to provide an instance of federation as a continuing contract, there are many more federations (e.g. the USA, Switzerland, Yugoslavia, India and so on) where no similar case can be made — where no 'foreign' power performs an arbitral function parallel to that which the United Kingdom can be held to have performed *vis-à-vis* the Canadian constitution. Secondly, assuming (as do most observers) that the accepted convention in British-Canadian constitutional dealings was for the British Parliament merely to rubber-stamp any proposed amendment duly and properly enacted by the Canadian Parliament, then to this extent the arbitral role of the United Kingdom would have been only formal, not substantive. Third, at the point where the Canadian constitution is or was 'patriated' — Canada in this being formally accorded by the British Parliament full control over its own amending procedures — then no grounds remain for regarding the Canadian federation (or 'confederation') as an ongoing contractual arrangement in the sense stipulated.

We next move on to take a_2 and b_2 together. In these two cases we are concerned with arrangements whereby a contractant is not just a party to a contract, but is also its authoritative interpreter or police enforcer (or both). The entrenched arrangement between component territorial units and the centre in a federation is of a kind where the centre, as one of the parties involved, has authority both to interpret and to secure enforcement of the constitution. It is for this reason that provisions a_2 and b_2 approach the federal reality more closely than do the rest.

There might, however, be some question as to the appropriateness of viewing such an arrangement as contractual. For it features one of several parties to an agreement being able unilaterally to interpret that agreement's meaning, to bind other contractants by this interpretation, and generally to determine the rights and wrongs of any conflict arising between himself/itself and these other parties. What is notable in any such arrangement is the absence from it of a significantly relevant equality among those agents designated as contractants — these, in an ongoing federation, presumably being identified as the federal centre, on the one hand, and the component territorial units, on the other. We need not necessarily contend that federations are in fact structured in this unilateral way. All we require to admit, where and if we project this sort of unilateral structure for federations, is that an important equality, normally taken to be relevant in any contract, is missing. For present purposes, the 'relevant equality' that we cannot detect is negative. And it would consist in the equal inability of any one of the contracting parties to interpret or to reinterpret or to enforce quite unilaterally its views and preferences upon the other contractants. Any agreement, which is not derived from compulsion, must feature relevant equalities among those agreeing. If a federal system — where the centre is sovereign and the component regions are not — is viewed as consistent with provisions a_2 and b_2, then of course a relevant equality between centre and locality is missing, such that the relationship between them could not convincingly qualify as 'contractual'.

Nothing in what has been said should be taken to imply that each territorial unit in a federation has no distinct identity *vis-à-vis* the centre. If the identities of component regions were not somehow distinct it would not be possible to entrench representation for them. Nor should it be understood that the component regions of a federation cannot in various circumstances bargain or negotiate with the federal centre. On the contrary, it happens all the time: often over national parks and reserves, economic development, cultural policy and so on. The important point, however, is that this distinctiveness of component regions is only partial; their independence is by no means entire; their equality of standing is incomplete; sovereignty they do not enjoy; they do not exercise control over locally resident citizens in a manner oblivious to the will of the centre; regional withdrawal is implicitly disallowed; and interpretation and enforcement of the constitution could be said to lie with the federal centre, or with the system taken as a whole, but certainly not with each component state, province, region, *Land*, canton, or whatever. If, despite all this, we insist upon regarding federations as contractual, then the expression may be admitted, but only presumably as some form of simile or metaphor.

Finally, we approach a_1 and b_1. There is really no need for elaboration here. As indicated, federations do not leave authoritative interpretation or enforcement of their constitutions to their regional components. Every sovereign federation contains properly constituted trans-regional judicial powers or procedures (sometimes including referenda) which provide a central and non-regional source for authoritative interpretation and enforcement.

There is no need to go on unduly about the contractual character of federal systems. In most cases, the intention is merely to suggest, by reference to the contractual simile, that federations are somehow 'democratic'. Indeed, federations *are* 'democratic', but only in the qualified way already suggested. And the qualification must extend to contract. Component regions and the federal centre do not, in any general way, stand on a relevant footing of equality *vis-à-vis* one another. Although there is usually some basis for bargaining between them, deriving from their partially distinct identities, there is no *legal* basis or prospect for a region ever to go it alone, to take its future into its own hands, should it prove dissatisfied with the mouse that protracted negotiations with the centre may often yield.

9 SECESSION NULLIFIED

Secession and Contract

One of the reasons why it is argued that federations are essentially contractual is because of the assumption that any contracting party remains as free to withdraw from, as it was to enter into, such an association — as for example in circumstances where the other party or parties violate(s) the terms agreed, or if the arrangement in other respects proves unfair or inadequate. John Calhoun perceived the American Union in this manner. Spokesmen today for a *Québec libre* (like René Levesque) perceive the Canadian system in similar terms (cp. Provencher 1977: 199–206; Mallory 1974; Cook 1969). The logic of this position is that federations consist of sovereign states. These constituent states in the nature of things, it is thought, cannot surrender their sovereignty. Where they pursue in concert with other states mutual interests, it is suggested that they enter into treaty arrangements, sometimes indiscriminately referred to as 'federations' or 'confederations'. One attribute of sovereignty is held to consist in the right of a state to adhere to its own interpretation of a treaty. The implication would be that no state member of a 'federation' or 'confederation' can ever be obliged to act in a manner inconsistent with its own reading of the treaty/constitution which defines its relations *vis-à-vis* other members. In as far as a 'federal' or 'confederal' associate is held only to be bound where it so chooses, this must imply that it enjoys a right, to use Calhoun's expression, of 'nullification' *vis-à-vis* those acts of the centre to which it takes exception — a right, in the end, which would have to encompass the even larger right of secession from the association.

Now whether or not federations, as Sidjanski (1956) states, enjoy a constitutional basis which 'excludes *any possibility* of secession' (p. 48, my italics) it is certainly true that federations do not at least in any way *provide* for it. Federations may well collapse, as did the Central African and West Indian federations (in 1963 and 1962 respectively). But then any state at all may disintegrate, as did a unitary Germany in 1945. These things are always possible. The question is whether such developments are intended and provided for. Federations, as indicated, certainly make no express provisions for secession. At least no federations we know of do this. (In the Soviet case, there is such a provision, but as will be shown later it is merely formal and is contradicted by other provisions.) Treaties invariably work within some time-frame – to expire at a given time, or to be reviewed at a given time, or more loosely to be reconsidered by either party at will and so on. Federations basically omit such considerations because the thrust of the new associative undertaking embarked upon directly contradicts them. Where a new federation is formed from originally sovereign states, things are not left as they were before, if for no other reason than that the citizenry of the states have acquired (or have had imposed upon them) a new, if additional, allegiance, which is to the federal centre, as similarly with the federal centre's assumption of a new, if additional, responsibility, which is to the citizenry of the states or *Länder* or cantons or provinces or whatever. Because of this integrated, if still differentiated, structure of federations, withdrawal by territorial units means (legally at least) much the same as collapse for the union as a whole. In all of the major states sometimes called federations – Switzerland, the USA, Canada, Australia, the USSR, India (post-independence), Brazil and so on – there has never yet been a successful secession. In Pakistan, Bangladesh successfully seceded only after a bloody civil war. In Malaysia, Singapore was expelled in order to avoid a bloody race war. But in Central Africa and the West Indies, the secession of some unit(s) in each case meant the disintegration of the union.

The important point is less that federal constitutions say they allow secession, or say that they disallow it, but that the structure of these governments is heavily weighted against it. The central government in a federation is not significantly distinguished from its constitutive member governments by virtue of its control over a distinct territorial zone (like Ottawa or Brasilia or Washington or Canberra), but by virtue of its exercise of distinct national functions which engage and affect the system as a whole. The exercise of these functions yields to the central government some partial authority over all citizens of the federation. A member state or province, by contrast, only exercises a partial authority over citizens who inhabit its territorial area. The effect, accordingly, of secession by a member unit is or would be two-fold. First, the local unit would consolidate its authority over the locality by excluding its national, central rival (such consolidation means nothing more nor less than the augmentation of its total power). Secondly, and as a part of this, the local unit would unilaterally eliminate the dual allegiance of its citizenry, replacing it with an integral duty to a single authority.

The central authority in an ongoing federation usually exercises control over certain officials dispersed among local authorities and always over the citizens of these localities. A central government which accepts secession by a local government, or which accepts that degree of local autonomy which is tantamount to the same, simultaneously accepts the extinction of any reciprocal duty between itself and its own citizenry in the affected locality. This is of course something that can happen to any central government, but it is not a matter which may be comfortably or coherently provided for in any constitutional arrangement whose precise purpose is to secure union — whether highly centralized or decentralized — on an enduring basis.

The Soviet constitution, which describes itself as 'a federal state', formally reserves to every Union Republic 'the right freely to secede from the USSR'. The USSR's is the only federal constitution to do this. Lenin, on 15 November 1917, proclaimed secession to be the inalienable right of all member nations of the system. Stalin agreed. And this pledge was renewed in the latest Soviet constitution of 1977 (Article 71). It is not surprising to discover that the rationale of this provision is essentially the same as that expressed by Calhoun. When the 1924 Soviet constitution was re-drawn in 1935, Stalin opposed the deletion of the article guaranteeing a right of secession. His argument? 'The USSR is a voluntary union of Union Republics with equal rights. To delete from the constitution the article providing for the right of free secession from the USSR would be to violate the voluntary character of this union' (in Riha (ed.) 1964, vol. 3: 625). The point Stalin was to make to the Seventh Congress of Soviets (1936) was that there was 'not a single republic in the USSR that would want to secede' anyway and thus that the question was in fact 'of no practical importance'. Whether or not union republics really wish to secede, the fact is that they have no effective means of doing so. This consideration requires account to be taken of substantive factors, like the predominant power of the Communist Party, and severe restrictions on the free flow of information. There is — besides these factors — a purely formal inhibition, internal to the Soviet constitution.

The intent of the secession-right was conditional, to the effect that secession was permissible if consistent, in Stalin's words, with 'the interests of the proletarian revolution' but not where (in Trotsky's words) it 'became a weapon directed against the proletarian revolution'. On this view, then, even were a constituent republic somehow permitted to bring itself to the point of formally demanding the right to secede, it would still remain the right of the Soviet Union to accede or not to the demand. The Soviet Union, through the Praesidium of the Supreme Soviet, is entitled to limit the sovereignty of member republics in numerous spheres. Were there any secessionist demand, this could be constitutionally ruled out as inconsistent with other fundamental provisions, such as that to do with 'safeguarding the security of the state' or that 'most heinous of crimes' involving the citizen's 'violation of the oath of allegiance'. The Soviet Union is of course very highly centralized. The right to secession featured in its constitution is formally on offer. But other provisions in the constitution leave it fully open to the centre, in effect, to decide whether any proposed secession should be allowed or not.

There has recently been a great deal of discussion in Canada about the possible secession of Quebec. It has been suggested, should popular opinion back René Levesque in his quest for provincial autonomy and independence, that the federal centre should concede this. Discussion has also moved, however, towards considering the possibility of incorporating a right of provincial secession into the Canadian constitution. The parallel with the Soviet Union is rarely touched upon. But suffice it to say that a secessionist provision, such as that supplied by the Soviet Union's Article 71, could of course be written into the Canadian or any other constitution (whether a federation or not). A precedent has been alluded to in the case of Sweden's historical union with Norway, where the latter was allowed to secede from the former in 1905 following a referendum — the Swedes putting behind them recourse to war. The fact is that Norway's course of action was effectively unilateral. It was heartily and unitedly supported by the Norwegian people. In view of the certainty of a destructive civil war were firmer action taken, the referendum agreed by Sweden can only be seen as a palliative which served to justify a result which probably could not have been averted anyway. What happened between Sweden and Norway, moreover, is not very different from what has happened elsewhere in a long line of secessionist or independence crises as between imperial centres and their colonial dependencies — whether it be a case like that of Eire breaking away from Britain (1922) or of Guinea breaking away from France (1958).

From the British perspective, whatever violence may have been employed on the Irish side to achieve independence, the Irish Free State Agreement Act was and is perceived as a concession voluntarily engaged in by the Parliament at Westminster. Guinean independence, from the French perspective, followed from a referendum voluntarily agreed, supervised and accepted (in its result) by De Gaulle's France. What has happened in France, Britain, Sweden and in so many other states, as regards component territories breaking away from metropolitan centres, might conceivably happen also in Canada *vis-à-vis* Quebec. But this is not a development which the present Canadian constitution provides for. If Quebec does secede and the Canadian centre does concur in such secession, this would almost certainly be done on the assumption that the cost of energetic intervention by Ottawa would in the end prove too high and perhaps self-defeating. Finally, even if a formal provision were written into the Canadian constitution detailing a procedure to be followed by intending secessionists, other provisions in the constitution which dictate federal responsibility towards all citizens in all provinces could still be used to undercut the utilization of such a provision — if the federal government concluded that it enjoyed a more than even chance of winning at small cost in any secessionist conflicts that might ensue. In any event, the structure of federations, as of all states, pushes them towards the retention of some form of unity. A formal provision opening up the prospect of a retreat from this objective would be inconsistent with it. Such a provision could be incorporated, as in the Soviet case, for the sake of appearances and out of a false regard for ideological 'consistency'. Or it could be incorporated as a frank admission of immediate or looming defeat for the prospect of continuing union — as in the case of the Swedish collapse before the fact of Norway. Either way, federations are no more consistent with secession than are non-federations. Equally, federations like non-federations may as readily be torn apart. But it seems unlikely that a constitutional provision formally admitting the possibility of secession would of itself have much effect either way.

If a federation's component territorial parts are implicitly entitled to secede in any effective sense, then the federal centre can only adopt and implement policies with the express or tacit concurrence of each member unit. If, however, the component parts are not entitled to secede (effectively, not formally), then they are equally unable unilaterally to veto or block or void the initiatives of the federal centre. The component territorial units of a federation are understood to be structurally incorporated into a single, coherent decision-procedure, not to enjoy an independent power to negate that procedure. In as far as the member units of a federation are effectively denied the right to secede, they are in this made subject ultimately to the decisions of a higher federal authority, whether this be the federal legislature or judiciary or executive or even popular referenda — and possibly of all these together. That the constituent territorial units of a federation are denied full sovereignty does not of course imply that they are denied an entrenched role in the exercise of such independence and sovereignty as is wielded by the federation as a whole. (For analyses consistent with

.that offered here, see Borel 1886, Le Fur 1896 and Nawiasky 1920.)

Federations are so structured as to preclude any effective right to secession — save perhaps formally and thus inconsistently or through inadvertence and practical incapacity at the centre. In this respect, federations are no different from any other states, including those customarily designated as 'unitary'. To say that the non-sovereign states of the member territories of a federation enjoy no effective entitlement to secede does not, however, imply that these member territories are denied all forms of autonomous interaction with foreign states — up to and including a treaty-making power. Units of a federation may well enjoy some capacity to act in the international arena independently of the federal centre — as in encouraging foreign investment or settling difficulties with neighbouring (but alien) provinces. This capacity, however, derives from the federal constitution, or some construction thereof, which permits member units to act in this independent manner; it will not derive from the sovereignty of the member units. The federal constitution may permit such independence of action, and such independence may in turn be recognized by the international community. As Bernier (1973) puts it: 'if the federal constitution grants [localities] the right to deal separately with foreign states and such states agree to deal with them, then they are subjects of international law' (p. 82). But being a subject of international law is not the same as being fully sovereign, which is the province of the federation only. 'In international relations, federal states are universally regarded as fully sovereign entities, notwithstanding any limitations imposed by their constitutions; as a result they enjoy complete international personality' (Bernier: 29).

Secession and Co-ordinate Powers

We have reviewed and rejected the theory of contract or of compact where this is taken to mean that federations confer upon component territories an effective right of secession. There is, however, a closely related notion which must be addressed separately. This is the view that component territories enjoy a 'co-ordinate' power with that of the federal centre. This notion has been expressed by a great many writers, although it is not nearly so fashionable as it once was. It may be formulated directly in terms of 'the establishment of a single political system, within which general and regional governments are assigned co-ordinate authority such that neither level of government is legally or politically subordinate to the other' (Watts 1966: 13). Or it may be formulated alternatively in terms of 'the principle of *duality* articulated in a single constitutional system of two distinct governments, national and state, each acting in its own right, each acting directly on individuals, and each qualified master of a limited domain of action' (Davis 1978: 114). The second formulation creates marginally less of a difficulty than the first; both are suggestive of the analysis provided by Kenneth Wheare (1946).

This view of federation as involving a duality or co-ordination of sovereign power between central government and member states is not recent — popular assumptions to the contrary. It is essentially an eighteenth-century innovation, the view originally set out in fact in *The Federalist* (1788). Davis (1978) expresses doubts about the originality of federation (pp. 114–19), but none the less regards the notion of duality formulated in *The Federalist* as new. The idea that federations involve dual sovereignty (which is all that the notion of a co-ordination of sovereign powers implies) was challenging because it attacked the more widely accepted doctrine that sovereignty was indivisible. Even Alexander Hamilton, one of the authors of *The Federalist*, suspected that this dual arrangement was not really tenable and he leaned towards a more monarchical system. John Calhoun, a pre-Civil War American Secretary of State, also assumed that duality was untenable. He did so, first on the grounds that the member units retained full sovereignty and, secondly, on the grounds that there was a compulsion on the part of the central government always to usurp that sovereignty. Alexis de Tocqueville (1835) affirmed this notion of duality, as did John Stuart Mill (1861) and A.V. Dicey (1885 and 1915). Harold Laski saw federation as offering a practical, if not a theoretical, triumph over the classical doctrine of sovereignty. This dual or co-ordinate sovereignty notion is not absurd. But neither is it tenable (as witness some of the arguments against it marshalled e.g. by Livingston, originally 1952, published in Meekison (ed.) 1971; Duchacek 1970; even Davis 1978; Riker 1964 and 1975).

The classical doctrine of sovereignty held in part that a sovereign state could have only one centre and that the power of that centre could not be divided. Any notion of dual or co-ordinate sovereignty was taken to violate this maxim. The Swiss scholars E. Borel (1886) and L.E. Le Fur (1896) so understood matters. They confidently drew the conclusion, based on North American and European experience, that federations enjoy a sovereignty fully assigned to their central governments and not shared by member states. Borel, for example, insisted that the duality of power signalled by Tocqueville was untenable. He pushed the case for attributing full sovereignty to the federal centre, arguing that the central government exercises an undivided and absolute power *vis-à-vis* its member states. Observers like Borel and Le Fur were basically correct. The trouble is that they paid too much attention – as did Bodin and Hobbes moreover – to the principle of indivisibility of sovereign power, as opposed to the more relevant mark of finality. It is not so much that sovereign power (in a federation or elsewhere) requires 'unitary' – in the sense of a single – authority, but that it requires a coherent decision-procedure. If the mark of sovereignty were a single authority then of course it (or he or she) could not be divided. But if the mark of sovereignty is finality of decision, then clearly such sovereignty can be divided among and be shared by (as in any voting situation) a plurality of agents – without prejudice to finality. In the case of federations, the 'centre' has to be understood as a coherent decision-procedure which incorporates into itself in various ways the constituent territorial units for purposes of ultimate decision-making. Once this is established, it becomes perfectly feasible to hold the federal centre to be sovereign, without construing this to mean that this coherent power of the centre absolutely excludes the participation of the 'periphery'. It is for this sort of reason that one requires, in any analysis of federation, more a theory of 'constitutionalism' than of 'democracy' – as a framework which pays due attention to procedure, not just to personae.

It has been consistently urged, against theories of duality and equally against philosophies arguing for local autonomy, that federal states incorporate procedures whereby member states can be overruled. Duchacek (1970) observes for example that all federations 'authorize some degree of central interference in the domestic affairs of the component units' (p. 275); that although 'federal constitutions recognize and pay due respect to two separate jurisdictions', their respective powers none the less 'are not and have not been meant to be equal'; that the 'national power is clearly favored' (p. 233). Indeed, every federation, in this respect, contains within itself the legal seeds for development into a more unitary system. A federation may well have an article in its constitution, as in the American case, which enjoins that 'no state without its consent, shall be deprived of its equal suffrage in the Senate' (Art. 5). But in the USA, all constitutional amendments require ratification by three-quarters of the states. It is unlikely, at this point in time, that it would happen, but it is clearly constitutionally possible that Article 5, entrenching equal representation of the states in the Senate, could be changed by following the stipulated procedure governing amendments. And the same may be said regarding the legal possibility of further integration within any federation given that there is always one or some procedure permitting member states to be over-ruled — whether or not it proves substantively possible at any given time to mobilize that procedure. There is no legal power which can absolutely prohibit a federation from eroding the entrenched position of its constituent units. One need only observe that, if that erosion is ever completed, the system simply ceases to qualify as a federation.

Where a federation is said to contain truly *co-ordinate* spheres of authority, with both central and local governments autonomous in their separate spheres, it is implied that neither intrudes upon the other, that neither is subject to the other, and that each has final say in its own domain. The sense of 'co-ordinate' most relevant to the present discussion is that which affirms 'an equality of rank or importance'. If the constitutive territorial units of a federation are regarded as equal in rank and (more vaguely) in importance to the central government, then presumably they can never really be subject to the 'central' government. Where any conflict supervenes, it must impliedly remain open to any equal party to withdraw. If the central government in a federation cannot, whether through its courts or otherwise, check or overrule in any way its 'subordinate' or 'local' counterparts, then the latter are presumably juridically entitled to perform as they like with respect to the centre — and certainly to secede from it. If subordinate or local governments *can* unilaterally secede from the centre, then in such degree are they neither 'subordinate' nor 'local', but properly equal instead, and possessed of their own centres. The possession of such a capacity for autonomous action effectively renders a government independent or sovereign. Federations, however, do not envisage secession, even if on occasion their populations should prove too disparate and their struc-tures too loose to prevent it. It is because federations are hierarchical, always concerned and usually able to exclude secession as an option available to *Länder*, *Ständer*, states and provinces, that it is inappro-priate to speak of such local units as enjoying a co-ordinate power.

The basic document of a federation — or constitution — will advance the duties either of the central or of the local government. If the docu-ment states the duties of the central government, it will generally be contended that all remaining or residual duties redound to the local governments; if local government duties are stated, it may be contended that all residual duties redound to the central government. There may, of course, be compromises between these two positions. But the basic assumption, whatever the compromise position, would be that *terri-torial* units (even where they represent or protect ethnic or professional or functional units) constitute vested interests which, beyond some point, cannot be infringed. This consideration is, of course, consistent with a right of secession from the federation. But there are contrary considerations.

The federal centre, whatever the duties directly or indirectly assigned to it, is assigned such duties on behalf of all citizens of each of the component territorial units of the federation. If a territorial unit rebels and, more than this, successfully secedes, the effect is to prohibit the federal centre from carrying out its duties *vis-à-vis* any of the citizens of the affected territory. Residents within a secessionist province, whether they wish it or not, may suffer some disruption or modification of family, commercial, social and other traffic with parts of the former union – all contrary to their former status. They may be made liable to new taxes, restrictions, conscription and even be directly mobilized to oppose the body or rump of the union. It does not altogether matter that a majority within a secessionist region shall normally support the secession. For the initial secession not only raises the question of entitlement by other regions in turn to their own secession, but more relevantly raises the question of the duties owed by the federal centre to those of its citizens resident in the locality who resist having their relationship with the centre unilaterally abrogated by the secessionists. The local territorial unit may well plead its right to go as far as it need – up to and including secession – in order to enforce its will in any jurisdictional dispute with the federal centre. But the structure of federations is such that, where the locality resorts to secession to enforce its perceived right, the locality denies the federal centre any means of executing its constitutional duty as perceived by it and by some minority at least of those citizens who are settled within the secessionist locality.

If federation were based on the assumption that local and central governments were equally supreme and final *within their respective spheres*, then this would entail that the union was merely a treaty arrangement. The reason why federal governments are generally not regarded as treaty arrangements is only because they do not meaningfully countenance any right of local secession – the only ultimate weapon of self-protection that a local territorial unit can really have. Such a right can of course be conceded on paper, as in the Soviet Union. It can be demanded as a right, as in Quebec. It is not a right, none the less, which can be conceded in any clearcut or coherent way, legally speaking, within a federal union. For the central government is not only dealing with interest-bearing territorial units, but also with interest-bearing individuals. Constitutionally, in law, the federal centre owes a duty to both. The federal centre may conceivably admit a right of local units within a certain sphere to have final say — and by implication to secede. But when the cards are down, it must remain for the federal centre to decide between these rival claims, between the local right to secede, on the one hand, and the implicit demand — by some proportion of the local citizenry who oppose secession — that the centre not surrender its duty towards them. The centre might decide either way, as indeed might any other state, depending upon the balance of political forces actually in play. The important point is that, legally, whatever tacit or express undertakings may have been made to localities about secession, the actual granting of this remains at the discretion of the centre in all federations.

Some parcelling out of competences is of course necessary to any large-scale administration of human affairs. A city, county council or corporation which operates within a precisely allotted sphere, operates independently within that sphere. Competences assigned may be more or less rigidly held. But the ultimate question is: who decides disputes regarding what is the appropriate sphere of authority of a corporation, or board, or inferior territorial unit? If it is not the peripheral unit itself, but an organ of the central government, then one is dealing with a political or legal system that ultimately requires the centralized co-ordination of separate authorities. If secession is not legally or effectively envisaged, then all disputes must be settled within the union. Such is the basic position with federations, however loosely joined their parts may be.

It is of course always possible that some given region or province owing allegiance to a federation may prove able to break away from it, just as a locality might free itself from allegiance to any other form of state. But this, as in virtually any such case, would be tantamount to a political, not a legal, act. There may be no legal provision prohibiting constitutive territorial units from holding referenda on the level of preference among local citizens for withdrawal from the federation. There might even be a formal provision granting entitlement to secession. (The Soviet Union provides the only contemporary example available.) The point is that any formal move towards secession must at the least conflict with the formal duty of the centre towards those of its citizenry at the periphery who oppose the forcible transfer of their allegiance. In any federal constitution there will always be grounds for regarding any acquiescence in local secession by the federal centre as illegal — as an abrogation of its duty. It is for this reason that a right of secession cannot effectively be guaranteed under a federal constitution. If 'guaranteed', the concession must prove a qualified one. And this must leave it ultimately to the federal centre to determine whether these qualifications are applicable. Any locality which attempts secession always runs the risk — in all existing federations the near certainty — of being adjudged *ultra vires*, of acting 'unconstitutionally'. Secessionists within a federation always risk being adjudged (by some organ of the federal centre) as guilty of contravention of federal law by virtue of obstructing the federal centre in the execution of such duties as it owes its citizens in the secessionist zone.

Whether the federal centre moves to subvert such local independence, or by contrast accepts it as legitimate, must largely depend upon the actual balance of extra-constitutional forces in play. As a practical matter, a federal centre may not have the power to abort a secession. But there will rarely be any dispute, in international law, about its legal entitlement to do this, where it concludes that it can and should. A secession may well succeed, as did Jamaica's in 1961. But more commonly, the attempt has the effect of concentrating the power of the rest of the federation against that of the region attempting to secede — as in the case of the American Civil War of the 1860s and of the Nigerian Civil War of the 1960s. When Malaysia expelled Singapore from the federation in 1965, the expulsion only confirmed the overarching power of the federation (even if it itself were acting 'un-constitutionally'), not a unilateral entitlement on Singapore's part to secede. When Bangladesh, by contrast, won its independence from federal Pakistan in 1971, it could not do so without recourse to war, and the attendant loss of many thousands of lives. In the absence of any legally established secessionist procedure to follow, taken together with a reciprocal legal allegiance between the federal centre and the citizenry of every locality, it is always likely that attempted secession from a federation, as from any other state, will ultimately be declared illegal by the centre.

In sum, any view of federation which holds it to be characterized by a true duality or co-ordination of powers must ultimately assume that the constituent territories enjoy full sovereignty. This is so where duality or co-ordination is taken to imply equality, and thus that the constituent territories of a federation are not subject in any way to the federal centre. Given that the powers of the state or provincial units of a federation are precisely or broadly stipulated in the constitution, true duality must imply that it remains for the constituent territorial units themselves to declare what their duties are under the constitution. The implication must be that it is equally for the federal centre to declare what its duties are under the constitution. Given that centre and periphery may here conflict, it is to be presumed that, for such duality of power to be effective, the constituent territories must also be entitled either to 'nullify' relevant acts of the federal centre or simply to withdraw from the union — since withdrawal is the ultimate means by which one partner may protect its interests in equal dealings with another. This must imply an unquestioned entitlement on the part of constituent federal territories to secede unilaterally from the union at any point they consider such action appropriate. There are innumerable treaty arrangements, past and present, which accord such unqualified entitlement to constituent units. But in no federation, save the Soviet Union, is such an entitlement in any way alluded to. And in the Soviet Union, despite Article 71 of the 1977 Constitution, this entitlement cannot be said effectively to exist for reasons given earlier.

To avoid all possible confusion, it must be emphasized that the object of the present analysis is not to establish that regional units within federations — or any other states for that matter — *ought* not to secede. It is to be presumed that no uniform recommendation that pretends to validity could be offered on such a matter. In certain circumstances, specific attempts at secession would be perfectly understandable and even justifiable. The present point, however, is to establish that the structure of federations, following the convention earlier proposed for identifying these, is such that secession is inconsistent with them in a manner exactly parallel to that in which it proves inconsistent for all other sovereign states.

10 CENTRALIZATION BY DEGREE

We have proposed that federation be regarded as distinctively characterized by the entrenched representation of 'peripheral' territorial units
(i.e. of local or regional governments) at the union centre. Such a form
of government is quintessentially constitutional and juridical. It may
well be that this sort of arrangement is inspired on occasion by a desire
to disperse power. But it may be observed that most frequently (as in
the USA, Switzerland, Canada and Australia) the original object was to
place a check on power-dispersal and to provide a basis for a wider unity
— within the limits imposed by conditions like great size and cultural
diversity. Federation generically conceived has less to do strictly speaking with the dispersal of power than with the designation of local agents
to represent regional or territorial units at the federal centre. Such an
arrangement may sit well with the exercise of considerable power at the
periphery, but it is obvious also that it is in no way incompatible with
the loss of considerable power by local governments (not least in the
USA).

A federation may create greater centralization than previously existed
over the same area, as was the case with the United States when established under its present constitution in 1789. Alternatively, it may
create greater decentralization than previously existed within the same
territory, as was the case with the West German Republic when founded
under its present constitution in 1949. Federations then, when coming
into being, may be either centralist or decentralist. Further, they may
grow more centralist, as under America's twentieth-century Imperial
Presidency, or they may grow more decentralist, as with Canada in the
1970s and 1980s (in response to Quebec separatism). Although federations may be less politically centralized than non-federations (Australia,
for example, as compared to Kenya), it remains that federations may
also be more politically centralized than non-federations — as in the
case of the Soviet Union compared to Italy or of the United States
today as compared with imperial Britain at the close of the nineteenth
century or as with Switzerland compared to Lebanon (most dramatically in the period from 1975 up to the present).

A federation is best conceived as a *kind* of polyarchic constitutional
system, along lines specified elsewhere, and not more vaguely as a *degree*
of decentralization. Every federation will betray different degrees (and

121

also types) of decentralization. And no one particular degree of decentralization can be identified as differentiating federal from non-federal systems, apart perhaps from the polyarchic constitutional formula already indicated.

Hans Kelsen (1961) is one of the more eminent of those writers who has maintained that it is 'only the degree of centralization' that distinguishes a federation both from 'a unitary state divided into autonomous provinces' and from 'an international confederacy of states'. He maintains that, 'on the scale of decentralization, the federal state stands between the unitary state and an international union of states' (p. 316). What Kelsen means by a *centralized* state is one whose laws 'are valid throughout the whole territory over which it extends'. He means by a *decentralized* state one in which some laws 'will be valid for the entire territory . . . while others will be valid only for the different parts thereof' (p. 304). He regards the federal state as decentralized (p. 317), just like the confederal state (or alliance) – with the exception that the latter operates both legislatively and judicially according to the unanimity principle (pp. 319, 321).

Kelsen's formulation is awkward. First, he asserts both federations and alliances (confederations) to be decentralized. Secondly, he argues the difference between them to lie in the degree of decentralization. But while he tells us what he means by decentralization, as also what he means by federation (no discernible difference), he does not in fact locate the degree of difference that supposedly obtains between federations and confederations where both are regarded as decentralized. The only intelligible supplementary difference that Kelsen does locate between federation and confederation is a difference of kind – namely, in the constitutional notion of a confederacy being controlled by the unanimity principle, a principle he does not hold to be applicable to federations. Accordingly, Kelsen's intended distinction between federation and confederation as a *degree* of decentralization is merely asserted, the actual degree itself being neither clarified nor specified.

Secondly, Kelsen's formulation also omits any relevant distinction between federations and so-called unitary states. This is said on the assumption, given Kelsen's definition of 'unitary' or centralized states, that none of the latter sort will be found empirically to exist. That is to say, it seems improbable we should locate any state without some *de facto* local laws or practices tolerated or endured by the central government – practices peculiar to only some parts of that government's territory, and not to the whole.

We may now distinguish more generally between two distinct types of centralization. (a) There is centralization of the sort secured where there is only one organ entitled to legislate for a given territory. (b) There is centralization of the sort secured where such a single organ only produces, sanctions or tolerates legislation that is uniformly applicable to all groups and regions throughout its jurisdiction. As regards (a), there is virtually no state, not even tiny Liechtenstein (62 m^2) or Bermuda (21 m^2), which does not have subsidiary local governments with some capacity for independent action.

We repeatedly confront variable sources of law: legislative enactment, the administrative law of statutory bodies, the bye-laws of local authorities, judicial precedents, local customs and so on. We repeatedly confront, too, variable applications of law by reference to locale and community. In many or most Western states, legislatures enact tax laws which — whatever the design — have the effect of applying less severely to very rich communities than to those of middling income, and to church and charitable organizations less severely than to small business firms.

Certainly, virtually every country which we have been disposed to label 'unitary' (here meaning non-federal) has some laws peculiar only to certain of its regions or localities. Scotland, for example, is held to be an 'integral' part of Great Britain. So it is. Scotland none the less retains its own established Presbyterian Church, a partially distinct legal and educational system and a Secretary of State charged with the oversight of Scottish affairs in the British Cabinet. (Scotland also circulates its own banknotes.) China, huge as she is, contains 30 major administrative divisions (provinces, autonomous regions and municipalities). Each of these divisions — as with any local government — is in some respects and within certain limits empowered to make or impose arrangements peculiar to itself. Even France, which has traditionally served as the classic example of a 'unitary' state, retains its 38,000-odd *communes*, each with an average population of about 1,300, each run by an elected mayor with his supportive municipal council. However dependent the French communes may be upon the departmental prefects and their surrogates, these localities none the less pass a variety of laws which often produce significant variations between communes in local taxes, water rates, parking laws, traffic laws and amenities of various kinds (pools, schools, public housing).

Virtually all imperial systems, very few of which have been 'federal', apply different laws to different territories or regions. The Roman Empire did not impose uniform regulations on Egypt and Britain, nor the Ottoman Empire upon the Maghreb and the Levant. The Portuguese,

British, French and Belgians did not govern their overseas territories by precisely the same rules, obviously, as were applied at home. The American revolutionary cry − no taxation without representation − reflected a popular awareness of non-application of uniform laws by a 'unitary' metropolitan legislature. The fact that a system may cease to be called imperial does not necessarily mean that the substantive relationship is changed. Following the close of World War II, the bulk of France's colonies were legally incorporated as integral parts of the Republic. The inhabitants of all of these areas were formally accorded the status of citizens, as opposed to subjects. This did not inhibit the passing of a non-uniform statute which secured that large numbers of colonials could only return small numbers of representatives, with small numbers of metropolitans returning large numbers of representatives. French Black Africa, for example, in the period 1946−60, constituted over 42 per cent of the entire population represented in the National Assembly. But Black African deputies constituted only a little more than 5 per cent of the Assembly's membership. The elaboration of an even more unitary French system from 1946 did not abolish the promulgation of differential laws for different parts of the system. Variations of this and other kinds may and do occur in all systems, whether or not they call themselves imperial. Authorities may not pay too much attention towards, or even try to deflect attention from, these variations: they risk being rounded upon as undemocratic. But these variations within 'unitary' states, whether styled undemocratic or not, remain a fact of political life. (Sidjanski 1956: 52 and 55, also argues against Kelsen's degrees-of-decentralization criterion for federation.)

One of the most recent advocates of federation as a degree of de-centralization is W.H. Riker (1975). He argues that we may place 'all governments on a continuum with respect to centralization' (p. 101). As with Kelsen, he distinguishes between confederations (Riker calls them 'alliances') and 'unitary' states (which Riker calls 'fully central-ized governments') − in order to situate federation between the two 'extremes'. Riker intends by alliance an arrangement in which the centre 'cannot make any policy decisions without first consulting all the member governments'. The implication is that an alliance is an arrangement in which the centre requires the support of every member unit before it can act, and that the unitary state or empire is one in which the centre requires the support of no member unit before it can act (a 'government is an empire in the sense that the rulers of the constituent governments have *no* political self-control'). It is between these poles that Riker places federation: an arrangement under which rulers can make decisions 'in only one narrowly restricted category' without the approval of member units, or one in which rulers can make decisions in all such spheres — minus one — without the approval of member units.

Essentially the same difficulty confronting Kelsen re-emerges. Just as there appears to be no government from which all territorial variation in the law is absent, so there would appear to be *no* government under which it would be possible to banish *all* forms and degrees of self-control among those subsidiary agents, bodies or units which are essential to its functioning. This must suggest, in a most important sense, that no 'fully centralized government' does or likely can exist. Riker implicitly admits this at those points where he states that a fully centralized government need only make 'basic' policy and that such 'a fully centralized government' may live with 'a great deal of administrative decentralization'. Clearly, if such a system is largely 'decentralized', it must admit of *some* degree of 'political self-control' among subsidiary units. If then there is no government which can be said to be 'fully' centralized, and if federations are only characterized as having a degree of decentralization, then one is left with no effective means of distinguishing between supposedly unitary states and federations. Federations do not reserve in any absolutely reliable way at least 'one narrowly restricted category of action' to member governments. This is so on the assumption that no member government of a federation is itself empowered to make final decisions about its own sphere of jurisdiction and because none is empowered to secede where its views fundamentally conflict with those of the centre. Hence the degree of decentralization which Riker falls back upon to distinguish federations from unitary states or empires evaporates — although he presents the case for it more attractively than previous writers.

There are no governments in which one body or person creates every rule and in which every rule is applicable to every social group or region or locale. Presumably, too, there are no governments, in as far as it is reasonable to call them such, which can be completely decentralized. Accordingly, the only states or governments we shall know will be both partially centralized and partially decentralized. Once the absolute extremes of centralism and decentralism are ruled out (it would suffice, however, to rule out the 'fully centralist' extreme), the problem is to determine whether federations can be reliably and distinctively slotted in as occupying a particular degree (or range) along a scale of centralism/ decentralism. We know that federations are not absolutely unitary. But then no state is. The whole idea of a 'unitary' state would appear something of a myth. We know, too, that federal states are not absolutely decentralized. Federal states, after all, are sovereign systems; every sovereign has some species of centre; and to have some sort of centre is logically incompatible with the notion of having none − the chief idea involved in the notion of absolute decentralization. The main problem that we face, then, where we seek to distinguish federations from other states by reference to their intermediate degree of decentralization, is that any state at all can be spoken of in these terms − as hovering between the abstractions of total and no centralization. To identify 'no centralization' with a unanimity principle of decision-making, moreover, is misleading since unanimity, where achieved, is itself an instance of concerted action − representing one type of centralization. A legislature, for example, which passes a measure unanimously is no less centralized than where it does so by majority vote.

It is important to recognize also that the characterization of federation as a degree of decentralization equally involves characterizing it as a degree of centralization. The one is inversely proportional to the other; each in this sense may be converted into the other. To describe federation as a degree of decentralization does not therefore preclude the apparently contrary operation of describing it as a degree of centralization.

If we are disposed to describe federation as generally decentralist, taking account of a supposed empirical tendency, then we shall encounter the obvious difficulty presented by so many federations (e.g., the USA, India, Switzerland, Australia) moving in the other − that is a more markedly centralist − direction. The point is not that we cannot speak of governments as marked by degrees of centralization/decentralization, but merely that we cannot say − or that no one has said − anything very reliable or distinctive about federations in this regard.

It is basically due to such failure that Davis (1978) has concluded that the distinction between centre and regions 'within each federal system varies constantly and markedly' and that 'the relationship between the center and the parts, in every federal system, has never consisted of one kind of interaction or one kind of interdependence' (p. 150). In short, there is no observed degree of centralization/decentralization which commonly and distinctly marks off federations from so-called unitary states or empires. To say, however, that degree of centralization/decentralization does not serve as a reliable and distinctive index of federation, is not to say that no reliable indicator is available.

W.S. Livingston (in Meekison 1971), like Kelsen and Riker, is attached to the concept of federation as a degree of decentralization. He asserts that all countries fall 'somewhere in a spectrum which runs from what we may call a theoretically wholly integrated society at one extreme to a theoretically wholly diversified society at the other' (p. 24). Livingston, it will be recalled, argues that federation has to do with 'differences ... of degree rather than of kind', as a 'relative' and 'not an absolute ... term'. Livingston fails to specify *what* degree of decentralization distinguishes federal from non-federal societies. Nor does he indicate what it is that federation is relative to. This failure, given the previous discussion, is what we should expect. We re-direct our attention here to Livingston, however, for the reason that he is concerned with federation, not as a degree of *governmental* integration, but rather as a degree of *social* integration.

Livingston argues that federation has a legal character, but that its 'essential nature' is not to be sought 'in the shadings of legal and constitutional terminology, but in the forces — economic, social, political, cultural — that have made [its] outward forms ... necessary'. Livingston regards federation as a solution to a problem, and thinks that to understand the effect one must grasp the cause. To put the point briefly, Livingston sees the form of government as a response to the underlying shape of society, so that his focus is more upon federal societies than upon federal governments. A federal society, for Livingston, is one in which language, ethnicity, religion, class, race, distance and so on differentiate and group its members on a territorial basis. But it is also one, he argues, in which these diversities are not 'so great that there can be no basis for [political] integration'. Like Livingston, R.L. Watts (1966) also thinks federations to be produced more by the underlying social infrastructure than by any formal constitutional superstructure, but that these superstructures, once erected, may subsequently influence 'social loyalties, feelings, and diversities' (p. 16). Despite qualifications, Watts regards Livingston's model of a spectrum of *societies*, ranged in degree of territorially based integration, to be useful (p. 95).

It is one thing to say that a society is 'federal' in the sense that its major linguistic, cultural, ethnic, economic or other interests are territorially grouped. It is another matter to say, given such grouping — which is in some degree present everywhere — that a particular type, degree or pattern of group alignment by territorial location will objectively cause or politically (morally) warrant the setting up of federal government. Both of these are interesting questions which could repay some empirical and contextual study in most countries. A concern with these questions must, however, lead us more directly into the analysis of 'cross-cutting pressures' or cleavages which is a subject better dealt with as a part of a general study of pluralism. Broadly speaking, a concern with functional interest groups may give rise to the institutional device of proportional representation, whether within a federation or not. Similarly, a concern with the representation of territorially based interest groups may give rise to the institutional device of federation. Every society has as components distinct functional groups, all of which must have some at least exiguous territorial base (if only as office space). If federations can be said empirically to emerge only after some particular degree of territorial basing by interest groups has been attained, it cannot be said that anyone has reliably identified the degree supposedly involved. What is none the less clear from this is the ideological continuity between pluralism and federalism as families of ideas. It is equally clear that talk about the 'balance' and 'equilibrium' of social forces — where this is meant to mark that point on the scale of social integration/disintegration which might generate the parturition of federal union — is hopelessly vague.

We may be concerned with the degree of decentralization which supposedly marks a federal government, or with the degree of disintegration which supposedly marks a 'federal' society. Either way there are serious difficulties. These difficulties are less trying, however, in relation to the concept of federal government than to that of federal society. We may think of a government as having fairly precisely assigned functions, functions which may be concentrated upon one person or body, or spread over several. We should be entitled to measure — formally, in the first instance — the degree of governmental decentralization/centralization by reference to the number of spheres subject to the control of the single (or several) ruling agent(s) or body(ies). The difficulties associated with such a procedure are in fact considerable. But they are little enough compared to the difficulties involved in measuring the degree of 'social' integration displayed by a system. This is so chiefly for the reason that 'society' has no identifiable centre of the palpable sort displayed by a government; and although it betrays differential spheres and identities, few are so conspicuous as the ministries, legislatures and courts of a government.

In any event, whether we are concerned with governmental centralization or social integration, they come in many different forms, none of which can be readily reduced to any one common measure with the rest. Livingston (in Meekison: 25-6) and Watts (p. 111) seek to distinguish between different degrees of integration in both society and government. But the problem of incommensurability, even when observers are aware of it, is one they are often too readily disposed to wish away.

There are different types of centralization/decentralization, of unity/ disunity: political, economic, historical, national, religious, cultural, ethnic, racial, spatial, class, professional, together with myriad sub-varieties. Livingston may well ask which of two societies — one divided by religion, another by language — can be reasonably and meaningfully regarded as less integrated. It is significant that he does not attempt to answer his question. In a parallel way, it might be asked which of two societies — one goverened by a single party and opposed by trade unions (as in Poland in 1981), another governed by an ecclesiastical element and opposed by subsidiary national elements (as in Iran in 1981) — is more centralized or integrated. In every system there are degrees of distinct types of unity — military, religious, linguistic and so on. If these various kinds of unity are not all commensurable, and they are not, we cannot expect to say very much objectively and precisely about any general degree of unity characterizing a given system. To bother about the cut-off point between federations and other types of government in terms of the degree of centralization differentiating them ultimately involves a serious misdirection of concern. It is because of it that Duchacek (1970) raises (p. 243) such a maddening question (which he knows cannot really be answered) as to whether a central authority, which only enjoys a ceremonial power, amounts to anything more than a league; or the question whether a central government which exercises 99 per cent of the power wielded within the system can remain federal. Due to the ultimate incommensurability of the data involved, such questions cannot accommodate answers burdened with any pretence of exactitude. Hence one good reason for sidestepping them altogether. If one does not sidestep them, one may be led like Duchacek to embrace 'the infinite variety of the federal theme', the absence of solid definitional boundaries between federations and other states, and to perceive federation as a 'sieve that permits mutual interpenetration' between them all (pp. 274-5).

PART THREE

CONCLUSION

11 CLASSIFYING FEDERATIONS

Federations are conventionally contrasted with unitary states, on the one hand, and with confederations, on the other. As examples of unitary governments, cases like those of France, the United Kingdom, Italy, Kenya and Egypt are commonly cited. The basic principle underscored in all of these unitary instances is that each of them supposedly displays one supreme, ultimate and unified centre of authority. As examples of confederation, observers conventionally refer to the Achaean League (of Ancient Greece), the New England Confederacy (1643), the American Confederation (1781), the North German Confederation (1867) and the Swiss Confederacy (in existence from medieval times up to c. 1847). More recent, post-World War II organizations that might be instanced are the North Atlantic Treaty Organization (NATO), the European Economic Community (EEC), the Arab League and the Organization of African Unity (OAU). The basic principle underscored in confederations is that the centre is not sovereign — it holds its authority at pleasure from the constituent ('peripheral') units of the confederation.

The distinction between 'unitary' and 'confederal' states did not significantly exist prior to the emergence of federations. The Renaissance and post-Renaissance distinction, stressed so dramatically by figures like Jean Bodin, Thomas Hobbes and Benedict Spinoza, was simply that between sovereign and non-sovereign states. This normally involves a contrast between centralized states of a monarchical kind, on the one hand, and groups of states more loosely associated by treaty or allegiance ('leagues', 'confederations') on the other. The classical theory of sovereignty insisted that the hallmark of a 'well-ordered' or genuine state was the presence within it of some agent whose power was absolute, total, indivisible, illimitable and ultimate. Proponents of this theory of sovereignty, when first confronted with federation, were basically disposed to assume that the latter could not endure. When a later century reconciled itself to the durability of federal unions, it was necessary to rope them to a conceptual beast already overburdened. Hence the unitary/confederal/federal typology.

The absolutists of the sixteenth and seventeenth centuries provided us with a very clear idea — if not an altogether tenable one — about what they meant by sovereignty. The fact of federation suffered from the defect of not quite conforming to their axioms. Either sovereignty

133

was a wrong-headed theory, or federation was misunderstood where perceived as non-sovereign. In fact, sovereignty was in part wrong-headed, just as federation was in part misunderstood. It was quite natural then that observers should attempt to salvage the theory of sovereignty by recognizing federation on an *ad hoc* basis – as somehow falling between the being and non-being of a fully sovereign state. The trouble with characterizing federation in this intermediate way is that to do so reveals little of a precise and reliable kind about its actual character. It also undermines the classical theory of sovereignty without precisely locating the nature of the difficulty it involves. It is to be expected that a figure like Alexander Hamilton should have fretted that the American Union might not prove fully sovereign. It would be equally commonplace for a figure like John Calhoun, years later, to contend that it was not meant to be. The concern in the one case is that regions be accorded no entrenched status and in the other that the centre be given no final power independent of regional veto. It becomes a quite different matter, however, to describe a federation as not fully sovereign, nor fully confederal, but something in between.

Unfortunately, the unitary/confederal/federal (henceforth u/c/f) typology has never told us a great deal. It remains alive and kicking all the same, despite the advanced old age which has settled upon it. It might be said that *The Federalist* gave birth to u/c/f, that Alexis de Tocqueville served it as nursemaid, that A.V. Dicey sought to instruct it as a wise guardian should, and that Kenneth Wheare haltingly attempted to will its remains to the future. Watts (1966) is only one of many acute contemporaries who has been touched by this tradition as where he writes: 'what distinguishes federal from other forms of government is that neither the central nor the regional government is subordinate to the other as in unitary or confederal political systems' (p. 355). In this sort of formula, the federal centre is depicted as neither absolutely unitary (equals 'sovereign'), nor totally and confederally dependent (as in a 'league'). It is described as enjoying an intermediate degree of centralization between an association that is fully sovereign and one which exercises little or no independent initiative. There comes a time when an old dog should be eased out of its misery: so with the u/c/f typology.

The u/c/f typology appears ready-made, even obvious, but it has evolved almost insensibly only over the past two centuries. It provides a response to the broad question: 'Who is he who is not sovereign within the system?' It advises us in a general way that federation is neither sovereign nor the reverse. The u/c/f, however, provides a response to the more specific question: is the *central* government or the *local* (member) government sovereign?' The answers that u/c/f accommodates are as follows. (1) Where the central government is called sovereign, the system is said to be 'unitary'. (2) Where the local governments are called sovereign, the system is said to be 'confederal'. Under the u/c/f typology, it will be clear, federation is merely a residual category. Thus (3) where neither central nor local government is sovereign, the system is said to be 'federal'.

The u/c/f typology, as we have seen, presupposes a specific question. One may test the utility of the typology by reference to the answers it provides to that question. If we inspect a system, which we may out of convenience call a federation, and ask whether it is the central or the local government which is sovereign within it, and are offered 'neither' as a reply, we have a reply that is not an answer. 'Neither' does not enlighten us as to whether sovereignty lies with the centre *or* the locality. It is of course true that this reply, which does not directly indicate where sovereignty does lie, at least reveals that neither of the conventionally anticipated responses ('with the centre', 'with the locality') is applicable. And that is an advance. For in this we are at least put onto the scent of a misconception. To spurn this 'neither' is not to suggest, therefore, that it has no redeeming value – or that it is simply incorrect. If one were asked whether John Wilkes Booth was Lincoln's father *or* his mother, for example, one would accept 'neither' as an appropriate response. But it is the sort of response which, in itself, reveals nothing about the fatal intersection between Lincoln and Booth. It is less the reply which is at fault than the question – one conceived so restrictively as to exclude any hope of the subject matter being properly dealt with.

Before we inspect the inadequacy of the underlying question to which the u/c/f typology supplies a response, we must look more fully at the characterization which the u/c/f schema supplies. Federations are conventionally regarded as occupying some middle ground, holding the balance between tyranny and licence, absolutism and anarchy, between total centralization and unmitigated decentralization. It has happened that this 'neither, nor' approach to federation, by virtue of its express and implicit emphasis upon intermediacy and balance, has tended to take a quantitative twist. The chief theoretical problem over federation developed out of the concern to establish whether it was 'sovereign' or not. The theory of sovereignty, though comporting quantitative elements, most importantly involved – as in the notion of a highest or ultimate power – a legal criterion. But given that sovereignty was regarded as comporting absolute centralization (consistent with the notions of 'illimitability' and 'indivisibility') and given that federation did not meet this criterion, the move was easily made to identify federation with some *degree* of centralization — or indeed of decentralization. U/c/f then involves a significant implicit shift from a broader legal to a narrower quantitative criterion. It is in this way that federation ('neither, nor') escapes a distinct legal characterization while simultaneously appearing as some vague but still measurable quantum of power (a degree, even if unspecified, of decentralization).

One of the most important mistakes made in discussions of federation is to assume that the degree of centralization is a generally or universally simple, practical and useful criterion for classifying and assessing the operations of governments. Nothing could be further from the truth. We noted earlier the importance of incommensurability. We shall of course always on occasion be required to speak of greater or less centralization/decentralization. But centralization comes in myriad varieties, affecting myriad functions, which frequently conflict with one another. This incommensurability exists, first, on a practical level. Any government, for example, which attempts centrally to prohibit the circulation of certain desired commodities (perhaps books or records or alcohol or marijuana) tends in the very act to generate decentralized traffic in those commodities. A central government which attempts such control must simultaneously lose control — as of an effective capacity to tax those commodities which will have been forced willy-nilly into the 'informal' or interstitial economy, this economy becoming the preserve of those shadowy — often 'shady' - elements who surface to manage it.

The incommensurability exists, secondly, on a theoretical level. Assume: (1) a distinction between spheres and degrees of government control; (2) a necessary limit to the number of spheres (just as the number of ministries in any government is always limited); (3) a necessary limit upon the number of civil servants who can be paid to manage the system (i.e. a distinction between government and society); (4) but no limit upon the depth of activity available within any given sphere, no limit upon the prospect of ever more detailed control. Given these assumptions, then any shift of personnel and resources from one sphere (or 'ministry') to some other — to increase depth of control in that other — must have the effect of diminishing depth of control in the first sphere. Any assumption that there can be an absolute or total degree of control, at one extreme, and no control, at the other, within any human association — whether we call it government, society or something else — is simply mistaken. In as far as this is true, then all states will fall between these extremes — including federation. Which suggests that to describe federation in terms of such an undifferentiated degree of 'inter-mediate' centralization/decentralization is to make no intelligible distinction between it and other types of government.

Centralization, then, has been the chief criterion by reference to which federation has been categorized. It should be noted, however, that just as there are innumerable and incommensurable types of centralization/decentralization, so are there other criteria for the classification of governments, which criteria have nothing to do with centralization, and which are equally innumerable and incommensurable. Among the most commonplace criteria for the classification of governments would be representative character, responsiveness to popular sentiment, quality or size of leadership element, efficiency, respect for 'due process', type of economy, size of territory, social characteristics of population and so on. Because of our common opposition to absolutism, conjoined with the simplistic assumption that absolutism can be reduced to a certain degree of centralization, it has become a commonplace to associate federation, conceived as a degree of decentralization, with other criteria — for example, 'responsiveness to popular will' — which cannot be assumed to correlate with it. (It is often pointed out, for example, that too much decentralization may undermine the capacity of a government to respond effectively to expressions of popular will.)

In the most recent literature on federation, there has emerged a marked aversion to the notion that federation empirically and positively correlates with virtually any other criteria of governmental behaviour. Davis (1978) makes the point that we have no evidence to suggest that federal (as opposed to non-federal) states, are strong/weak, adaptive/maladaptive, flexible/rigid, conservative/progressive, legalistic/political (in conflict resolution), efficient/inefficient, for/against liberty, centralist/decentralist in disposition and so on (pp. 209–13).

These negative conclusions are, in fact, no more than we should expect — for the reason that we cannot meaningfully investigate the empirical correlates of federation without first establishing a coherent convention regarding what we are to have 'federation' mean. And the 'degree of decentralization' convention, which is that most widely accepted at present, is incoherent. First, it does not establish *the* degree of decentralization that would distinguish federations. Secondly, it does not stipulate the relevant spheres of decentralization supposedly involved. The upshot is that any system, on this criterion, can be 'federal', since they are all marked by some degree of decentralization in all spheres.

The trouble with the u/c/f typology is embedded in the classical theory of sovereignty. The reference to a supposed 'unitary' state only really involves an adjustment to the theory of sovereignty. The effect of the adjustment, however, is to render the whole concept redundant. At first there were only sovereign states and leagues (to put it simply). Then there were federations. Given the apparent difficulty of fitting federations into the category of fully sovereign states, federations were relegated to a third category. We have noted the difficulty with this third category – it being reduced to a 'neither, nor' status, acquiring in the process a vague but still quantitative character. However, an equally important problem arose in relation to the new (or re-named) 'unitary' category. Clearly, every government, conceived as a unit, is 'unitary'. This is merely a catch-all category, being less precise than 'sovereign', with its only virtue – and a doubtful virtue at that – being to exclude the newly emergent federations from its purview.

Even some of the most ardent proponents of the u/c/f typology are troubled by the vacuousness of the unitary category. Wheare (1951), for example, remarks that 'the class of unitary constitutions is so wide and varied, the degree and method of decentralization in practice in unitary constitutions is so diverse, that a good deal more must be known about a constitution described as "unitary" before we can feel we know what it is like'. The fact is that when one is told that a constitution is 'unitary' one is scarcely told anything more than that it does not *call* itself 'federal'. Wheare's reluctant conclusion was that the distinction's 'value is limited' (p. 30). On reflection, it is difficult to detect any value in it at all. Just as the u/c/f typology reduces federation to a quantitative criterion, so is the same achieved with regard to sovereignty. Under the u/c/f typology, the quality taken to be essential to sovereignty is 'indivisibility', and 'total' power so understood. A 'unitary' state is merely understood to be a 'sovereign' state where power remains undivided – one where there is the highest degree of centralization. But we cannot know what this highest degree would be. Moreover, there is no sovereign state whose power is not in some way, *de facto* or *de jure*, divided.

Kelsen (1961), like Wheare, accepted the u/c/f typology, attempting to rationalize it by reference to degrees of centralization. Kelsen regarded federations, across the board, as being quantitatively more decentralized than 'unitary' states. He expressed the quantitative difference supposedly involved only vaguely, in terms of the territorial components of federations enjoying a wider range of legislative initiative than the provinces of empires. Kelsen none the less concluded that there exists a great similarity 'between the structure of a federal State and that of a unitary State subdivided into autonomous provinces' (p. 317). A formal difficulty attaches to resolving the factual question. If one is to show that federations are similar to but less decentralized than empires, it will be necessary most importantly to stipulate the types or spheres of decentralization intended and also to say whether the type of decentralization in question is merely formal or genuinely substantive. (For example, a governor of a colony, like Sir Gordon Guggisberg in the Gold Coast, might *on paper* have been far more dependent upon the imperial centre in the control allowed over the development of the colonial economy and the pattern of taxation than would have obtained for the governor of any American state, while enjoying *in fact* far greater substantive independence in such matters than his American counterpart.) If, however, one does not wish to be so precise about the factual question, and advance to a rather coarse generalization, it would presumably be more correct to maintain that the federal USA in, say, 1970 was far more centralized — politically, culturally and economically — than was the 'unitary' British Empire in, say, 1920. In short, a system commonly called 'unitary', like the British Empire, might be less centralized in various respects than a system, like the American (at specified points in time), which is commonly labelled 'federal'.

The relevant option is not to discard (as hinted at by observers like Davis) the federal category, but to dispose of the 'unitary' category instead. The notion of a 'unitary state' is trivial in the sense that every state must be supposed in some sense to be unitary. The notion becomes absurd, moreover, because it supposedly excludes federations. We simply cannot say what a unitary state is, other than trivially or incoherently. If, however, we forget about the criterion of centralization/decentralization, we can say conveniently and accurately enough what a federal state is. To do this meaningfully we shall have to return properly to the problem of sovereignty. But let us say for now that the sovereign/non-sovereign typology is at least symmetrical. The u/c/f pretends to be but is not. The simplest solution is to regard federations as a subcategory of sovereign states, and not as a distinctly parallel category. Treaty organizations (leagues and so on) may be regarded, by contrast, as a subcategory of non-sovereign states. The notion of a 'unitary' state serves no relevant, useful or coherent purpose in all this.

We have already stipulated what a federation is. We shall now briefly rehearse and elaborate upon the position. A federation is a state which is constitutionally divided into one central and two or more territorial (regional) governments. The responsibility of the centre is nation-wide, while that of the territories (regions) is mostly local. The central government is not sovereign in a manner which excludes the involvement of the regional units. This is because these units are constitutionally incorporated into the centre for certain purposes, as to do with the way in which the centre's legislature is constituted or its executive appointed or constitutional amendments enacted. The sovereign element in a federation always consists accordingly of at least three or more bodies − that is the centre plus the two or more regional/cantonal/provincial/ state units. Political participation by persons resident within the two or more regional units, and at the regional level, may be restrictive and unrepresentative or representative and inclusive. While any regional unit, on the local level, may conceivably govern despotically, government at the national level, given a minimally triadic structure, is necessarily consultative − among those agents who constitute the sovereign element. To say as much does not exclude the possibility that the national government of a federation may rule by fiat over external elements such as colonies, or engage in or permit such rule over internal colonies, whether we call these 'minorities', 'nationalities', or something else.

A federation may be an autocracy in as far as it features an exercise of control over other groups whose participation it excludes. But we shall here consider it as a case of corporate self-rule, which is to say as some form of democratic or constitutional government. When we speak of democratic rule, we only establish a contrast with autocratic rule. Besides, there are different varieties of democratic rule. Federation is only one of these. Federations incorporate some division of labour between centre and periphery. But then so do all other governments. Federations might be said to establish such a division in greater degree than other democracies. But any emphasis upon some one degree to the exclusion of another must prove arbitrary. What we must therefore seek are differences of kind as between federations and other democracies. A federation, in securing finality of decision, not only takes account of individual citizens, but also of certain constituent territorial regions, affording them special representation in the decision-making procedure. This can be achieved by establishing a separate regional chamber within a bicameral legislature, or by providing each region with an equal set of extra legislators in a unicameral legislature, or by requiring the express assent − either unanimous or majoritarian − of regions to constitutional amendments, and it is presumably possible to achieve the same effect in other ways still. The business of affording special representation to the constituent *regions* of a federation in the matter of securing finality of decision is distinctive. Accordingly a federation may conveniently be defined as a constitutional system which instances a division between central and regional governments and where special or entrenched representation is accorded to the regions in the decision-making procedures of the central government.

The classical doctrine of sovereignty is, of course, far too absolutist to account accurately for the character of virtually any state, not just federation. It assumes that there is a sovereign in every system and that this sovereign consists in some one indivisible agent always to the exclusion of other agents within the system. The doctrine assumes the inescapability of rule by fiat, whether the ruler be one or many. It assumes finality of decision to be possible only where some distinct agent (single or plural) enjoys the authority to command the rest. It views order as a function of command and obedience. We have indicated that no agent ever enjoys all such powers: as of total, illimitable and indivisible power. This sort of observation none the less cannot be expected to cut much ice in circumstances – as in sixteenth-century Europe – where virtually everyone's ideal state was regarded as consistent with absolutist criteria. The classical doctrine only becomes acutely, dramatically anomalous at the point where a different ideal comes to be entertained: the ideal of democracy or republicanism. If a sovereign must, by definition, be absolute, unlimited, above the law and so on, it will obviously become difficult for a democratic state to qualify as sovereign. This will be so at least where 'democracy' is taken to imply a sharing of power, citizen participation in its exercise, and rule of law. The problem with the classical doctrine is readily spotted: it rules out as impossible what is for us real to the point of being common. In short, the position we are today entitled to hold is that a sovereign democratic state, in the degree that it is democratic, is necessarily bound by some rules which it cannot stand above or otherwise escape, and that it is in this sense necessarily limited. The power of a sovereign democratic state is not absolute, total or unlimited, but rather the reverse of all these things. Broadly speaking, all that we need say is that the procedure – and hence the power – of a democratic state is coherent and is in this sense consistent with the demand for finality of decision.

For various reasons, the classical theory of sovereignty is inadequate. If we are to regard federation as a form of sovereign state, it is necessary to indicate in advance what we intend by sovereign. We may stipulate a sovereign state to be a territorially defined unit which has established and coherent procedures for conflict-resolution and decision-making within its borders, which is neither legally subject to nor substantively bound by any other entity external to itself, and which has designated agents (e.g. rulers, civil servants, etc.) to act on its behalf. Such a definition as this excludes any consideration of absolute, total, illimitable or indivisible power as marks of sovereignty. It does not, however, exclude notions of rule-coherence, finality of decision, or political hierarchy. With such a definition, there remains no need for the concept of a 'unitary' state. A federation is merely one of many different, indeed innumerable, types of sovereign state which can be instanced – it being impossible, for reasons that we shall not here offer, to lay out all of the different types that might be adduced.

The most distinctive feature of federation is the entrenchment of regional components such that these are represented at – and in this sense constitute a part of – the national centre. I find it convenient to call such a structure *polyarchic*. A corporatist state which entrenches the representation of its professional groups at the centre, while not federal, is equally entitled to be called polyarchic. So with any league or confederation. The difference between a federation and a confederation – just as with that between federal and corporatist states – is not best dealt with as a matter of degree of decentralization, but in terms of a difference of organizational or legal or constitutional principle. In the federal/confederal case the difference is between one polyarchy whose decision-procedure is ultimately majoritarian as opposed to the other which operates basically on a unanimity principle.

Polyarchic states may be contrasted with *mono-archic* states, and both in turn with *acephalous* systems. The latter two cannot be dealt with here. Something further, however, must be said about the entrenchment criterion for federation. It is clear that no solution to one problem solves all problems. What is accepted at one point as a solution is transformed, at another, into a dilemma. This is not because truth is 'relative'. The reason is that every solution reposes upon unchallenged assumptions; some of these must prove inadequate or mistaken; and to spot any one of these inadequacies is to prepare the ground for a different solution or outlook and possibly a more comprehensive one. Some such transmutation may eventually be expected with regard to the stipulations about federation offered in this book.

For the moment, however, it is as well to ward off premature criticism in regard to the notion of entrenchment. Let us assume that all states, excepting perhaps the very tiniest, display *de jure* or *de facto* devolution or decentralization of some type and in some degree. Let us assume further that all representative states feature the representation of local elements in the decisions of the national centre. We may take it that 'representative' states are democratic in the degree that they are representative. We may also allow 'local elements' to encompass territorial, professional, religious, ethnic or any other sub-groups. The chief problems, then, with determining whether or not a state is federal lie in (a) establishing that the basis of its representation is territorial, (b) that this territorial representation has at least two tiers ('local' government and 'regional' government); (c) that at least the regional units are electorally and perhaps otherwise incorporated into the decision-procedure of the national centre; and (d) that the basis of such regional representation at the centre cannot be easily altered, as by resort to the bare majoritarian procedure which serves normal purposes: regional, territorial representation, in short, must be 'entrenched'.

If we take (a) through (d) as the criteria for entrenchment peculiar to federation, it ought in principle to be possible to decide any case that may be raised for inclusion. Suppose an observer, perhaps Duchacek (1970), were brought to conclude that the 'system of British government is in fact federal' on the grounds that 'the territorial division of authority in the United Kingdom' between Northern Ireland, Scotland, Wales and England was 'solidly guaranteed by a constitutional consensus without a written constitution and generally implemented in practice' (p. 121). If we test the status of the United Kingdom as a federation against our criteria, it will be clear that she meets only the first of these, while failing all the rest.

Hicks (1978), for example, implicitly invokes criterion (d) as a test of federal status. In effect, Hicks maintains that federations entrench the representative position of their state or regional components by contrast with non-federal states where 'lower-level governments are merely statutory bodies' subject to be swept away by the centre at any point or to have their position — which is not constitutional — eroded, as 'has occurred in the Netherlands, and may be occuring in the UK today' (p. 5). This erosion of course did finally happen in Northern Ireland after 1972. By contrast with federations, it only takes an ordinary parliamentary majority in the UK to reverse any statutory arrangement relating to the mode and scale of representation of component regions. It is not, however, a good idea to formulate this notion, as Hicks does — in effect following A.V. Dicey — in terms of 'the rights of the states' being 'guaranteed by the constitution'. Although Dicey's way of putting the case is neither incomprehensible nor absurd, it does land one with the inconvenient notion that an inert document — 'The Constitution' — nimbly and autonomously performs as an active agent. It is simpler to say that the regions (states, provinces, cantons) are constitutionally incorporated into the centre as an essential or entrenched aspect of the centre's decision-making procedure.

Obviously, such an arrangement can be altered. The regional components of federations are not sovereign. Ultimately, some form of coherent and integrated decision-making is available to the federal state taken as a whole. At the extreme, it is constitutionally possible for the federal centre to erode and even eliminate regional entrenchment — resorting the while to the extraordinary constitutional measures which would be required to accomplish this. We need not be distracted by discussions of co-ordinate, co-operative and organic federation, all registering some concern with degrees of growing centralization. The point is that a federation is a federation in as far as it meets the established criteria for it *qua* federation. But there is nothing to stop a federation, assuming it to be in all relevant respects sovereign, from eliminating the entrenchment of regional interests which distinguishes it from non-federal entities. How a federation evolves, in short — and it can evolve in any direction — is a quite distinct question from what it is *qua* federation.

If we are ever to provide intelligible comparisons of federations on an empirical basis, it is first necessary to stipulate quite clearly what it is that we intend by 'federation'. It is not enough to provide *examples* of federations. Unless we stipulate the principle(s) which these examples instance, we literally cannot know what they are examples of. A federation, unlike Mr Nixon, is not a body that one can kick around — not just any more, but at all. In this book, I have tried to provide a coherent stipulation. It is only from such a beginning that it becomes possible to attempt to determine what other correlations there are, if any, as between all systems which fit our federal criteria. To move to the empirical level only after first having a serious try at basic conceptual analysis of the key components involved in the hypotheses advanced will not of course guarantee sound results. But to omit such basic analysis will most certainly ensure misconception and muddle. Obviously, the 'federal idea' has no 'essential' meaning. But it will be equally obvious that it will have no coherent meaning at all — nor serve as a subject for empirical comparison — if we do not (a) analyse its variant normative thrusts and (b) establish at least some one or few, and hopefully narrow, criteria regarding fundamental aspects of its actual or empirical character. We require to establish a coherent convention which fits at least a great proportion of the facts, and to the extent that any working definition does this it will be plain that it will be more than merely 'arbitrary'. What is crucial is the prior importance of stipulating the nature of a federation as a logical or legal or constitutional *type*, well before one begins to try to measure it as a *degree* of decentralization or anything else. Such is the programme that has been attempted here. Once the type is stipulated, then the notion of federation will accommodate any degree of variation that remains consistent with the type (cp. Sidjanski 1965: 52, 55).

The beginning of any proper analysis of federation must be stipulative and the stipulation involved must be of a constitutional kind. In this respect, Dicey and Wheare were on the right path. One cannot leapfrog the process of conceptual identification, pell-mell, into the broad empirical conclusion. Where the prior focus is upon the kind of system a federation is, it cannot simultaneously be upon any one of the various degrees of integration (and integration of very different and sometimes contradictory kinds) that any federation might instance. Once we stipulate coherently and relevantly the kind of system we take a federation to be, we may proceed to investigate empirically such other correlations as may obtain between them. To speak of constitutional stipulations, one need only assume some notion of institutional arrangements sufficiently fixed and stable (indeed entrenched) to require some unusual or extraordinary procedure to overturn them, irrespective of whether these arrangements are written on paper or firmly imprinted on men's minds.

All political systems, including federations, can be viewed as characterized by a constitution, that is a basic controlling document or customary understanding – in as far as each provides in some degree for the non-violent change or renewal of leadership and thus for continuity and stability so understood. This will hold equally for an hereditary monarchy, the federal government of India and the Arab League. A constitution may, of course, be written, as in the American case, or unwritten, as in the British. But in either case, its character is such as minimally to indicate (or enjoin) the procedure which is assumed to be binding upon any present leadership in regard to the manner in which and the term for which (this may be life) successors are to be designated. Further than this, it may enjoin very little, or a very great deal. To place the discussion of federation in context, it is essential to investigate the basis of political typologies. To do this, some resuscitated concept of constitutionalism will probably prove essential.

12 POSTSCRIPT

The likeliest key to federation, to the distinctive character of federation
– conceived as an institutional reality – is not directly the promotion
of decentralization or centralization or a balance of powers, nor therefore any promotion of an abstract liberty or authority or balance
between these. The key to federation is its universal constitutional
attribution of entrenched powers at the centre to constitutive and non-
sovereign territorial units. This entrenched representation of territorial
(state, provincial, cantonal or whatever) units sometimes comes about
by reason of vast geographical extent, as basically happened in the
United States and in Australia. It is equally often resorted to because
of ethnic or other particularisms (as in Switzerland and India) where
these particularisms seek to defend themselves at the centre with the
help of a territorial base.

We have referred to federalism as ideology or philosophy and to
federation as institutional fact. Institutions remain human, all the same,
and must accordingly be governed by some one or several purposes.
For all of its institutional character, a federation is still governed by
purpose, and thus reflects values and commitments. When we portray
federation in terms of the entrenchment of territorial components,
we imply that the institutional fact involved reflects commitment to
entrenchment. Commitment is rarely, if ever, entirely without qualification. In federation, the entrenchment of regional power at the
centre will chiefly derive from centralist or decentralist motives and
will generate movement in either a centralist or decentralist direction.
And this direction can be, and equally readily is, discussed in terms of
establishing or restoring a balance, although not usually in any entirely
satisfactory manner.

Federation, while helping to solve some problems, is not a political
panacea. Just as federation is often promoted for reasons not entirely
sound, so may it be opposed in circumstances where its application
might prove highly appropriate. In our own time, there is considerable
argument for economies of scale, and for larger political entities to
exploit these. There is also considerable opposition to centralism arising
from fear of the destruction of local languages, cultures and identities
which such centralization may set in train. Wider union is in many
respects – global commerce, technology, manufacture, entertainment,

146

communication – already an achieved fact. Wider union on the political level is also in some degree necessary. The chief question is how best we might carry unification forward with the least harmful effect. Federation, in its centralist aspect – as in Australia, Canada, the United States, Brazil, the Soviet Union and elsewhere – has been in recent times the primary political device employed to promote unification movements. It is not farfetched to suppose that it shall continue so, quite possibly in Western Europe. Of all the continents, it is perhaps in Africa that greater unification is most necessary, given that Africa has the largest number of sovereign states in relation to area, as also the largest number of the world's least developed economies.

Political leaders may seek to establish or to maintain a wider union. They may equally seek to break away and set up shop on their own – or alternatively to break away and to forge links with another entity. In any case, one of our practical concerns must be to reduce levels of violence as far as we can, consistent with a respect for principles of justice. In some countries, the national centre may extend its authority in order to check the violation of civil liberties within some of its regions. In other countries, there will be a case for the national centre – whether old or new, prospective or actual – wielding less authority in the regions precisely because of the centre's present or potential insensitivity to the peculiarities, rights and needs of local peoples. In the second case, national leaders often oppose any legal recognition of territorially based particularities out of an understandable desire to strengthen the state and to prevent its dissolution. But equally understandably, local leaders often oppose union from fear that they shall suffer disproportionate economic loss or cultural humiliation or political oppression or all of these things.

Utimately, both the unionist and the secessionist usually offer their case as a defence of the welfare of the people. It can scarcely be argued, however, that this welfare is ordinarily served best by simple recourse to unbridled violence. Mainland China seeks to incorporate or reincorporate Taiwan; Ethiopia, Eritrea; Morocco, Sahara; Senegal, Gambia; Syria, Lebanon; Indonesia, West Irian and Timor; Vietnam, Laos and Cambodia; North Korea, South Korea (and vice versa). For a national centre to promote union on terms where the distinctiveness of local groups is entrenched, as potentially in a federation, may provide the only means of securing any fruitful union at all. For localities to accept the principle of closer union may well, in certain situations, have the effect either of encouraging economic development or of abating violence or both. What is almost certainly required today is greater respect for constitutional forms. The federal variety of constitutionalism, despite all of the misunderstanding often associated with it, does represent a coherent and tried expression of political sovereignty. When federation is properly understood, not only in terms of its inadequacies, but equally in terms of its advantages, we may anticipate perhaps greater recourse in future to it – not only as a means of extending, but equally of maintaining, political systems.

BIBLIOGRAPHY

Aitkin, D. (1977) *Stability and Change in Australian Politics*, Canberra

Albertini, M. *et al.* (1973) *Storia del federalismo europeo*, Torino

Althusius, J. (1603, 1614: 3rd edn) *Politica methodice digesta atque exemplis sacris et profanis illustrata*, Herbornae Nassoviorum

Amellier, M. (ed.) (1966) *Parliaments*, London

Aris, R. (1965) *History of Political Thought in Germany from 1789 to 1815*, London

Aron, R *et al.* (1958) *L'Ere des fédérations*, Paris

Aspaturian, V. (1950) 'The Theory and Practice of Soviet Federalism', *Journal of Politics*, 12, pp. 20–51

Awa, E.O. (1964) *Federal Government in Nigeria*, Berkeley

Ayearst, M. (1960) *British West Indies: The Search for Self-Government*, London

Bakunin, M. (1953) *The Political Philosophy of Bakunin: Scientific Anarchism*, comp. and ed. G.P. Maximoff, with an Introduction by R. Rocker, New York and London

Beck, J.M. (1971) *The Shaping of Canadian Federalism: Central Authority or Provincial Rights?*, Toronto

Bennett, W.H. (1964) *American Theories of Federalism*, University, Ala.

Bentley, A.F. (1908) *The Process of Government*, Chicago

—— (1967) *The Process of Government*, ed. P.H. Odegard, Cambridge, Mass.

Bernaus, A.J. (1966) *Federalismo y Revolución: las ideas sociales de Pí y Margall*, Barcelona

Berneri, C. (1922, 1976) *Peter Kropotkin: His Federalist Ideas*, Honley, Yorkshire

Bernier, I. (1973) *International Legal Aspects of Federalism*, London

Birch, A.H. (1955) *Federalism, Finance and Social Legislation in Canada, Australia and the United States*, Oxford

—— (1966) 'Approaches to the Study of Federalism', *Political Studies*, 14, 1, pp. 15–33

Bluhm, W.T. (1968) 'Nation Building: The Case of Austria', *Polity*, 1, pp. 149–77

Bombwall, K.R. (1967) *The Foundations of Indian Federalism*, New York

Borel, E. (1886) *Études sur la souveraineté de l'état fédératif*, Berne

Bowie, R.R. and Friedrich, C.J. (eds) (1954) *Studies in Federalism*, Boston

Brugmans, H. (1969) *La Pensée politique du fédéralisme*, Leyden

Brun, C. (1911) *Le Régionalisme*, Paris

Bryce, J. (1888) *The American Commonwealth*, London and New York

Brzezinski, Z. (1960) *The Soviet Bloc*, Cambridge, Mass.

Calhoun, J.C. (1851) *A Disquisition on Government and A Discourse on the Constitution and Government of the United States*, Vol. 1 of *The Works of John C. Calhoun*, Columbia, SC

Callard, K. (1959) *Political Forces in Pakistan 1947-1959*, New York

Camargo, P.P. (1972) *Los sistemas federales del continente americano*, Mexico City

Carr, E.H. (1937) *Michael Bakunin*, London

Carsten, F.L. (1959) *Princes and Parliaments in Germany: From the Fifteenth to the Eighteenth Century*, Oxford

Chanda, A. (1965) *Federalism in India: A Study of Union-State Relations*, London

Charvin, R. (1973) *La République Démocratique Allemande (RDA)*, Paris

Chopard, T. (ed.) (1963) *Switzerland, Present and Future: A Small Country Re-examines Itself*, Bern

Clark, J. (1938) *The Rise of a New Federalism*, New York

Clay, L.D. (1950) *Decision in Germany*, London and New York

Coleman, J.S. and Rosberg, C.G. (1964) *Political Parties and National Integration in Tropical Africa*, Berkeley

Cook, R. (1969) *Provincial Autonomy: Minority Rights and the Compact Theory, 1867-1921*, Ottawa

Cooray, L.J.M. (1979) *Conventions, The Australian Constitution and the Future*, Sydney

Creighton, D.G. (1964) *The Road to Confederation: The Emergence of Canada 1863-1867*, Toronto

Crépeau, P.A. and MacPherson, C.B. (1965) *The Future of Canadian Federalism*, Toronto

Crispo, J. (1979) *Mandate for Canada*, Don Mills, Ont.

Currie, D.P. (ed.) (1964) *Federalism and the New Nations of Africa*, Chicago

Curtis, L. (1915) *The Problems of the Commonwealth*, London

—— (1934-7) *Civitas Dei*, 3 vols, London

—— (1939) 'World Order', *International Affairs*, 18, 3, pp. 301-20

—— (1945) *World War: Its Causes and Cure*, London

Dahl, R.A. (1971) *Democracy in the United States: Promise and Performance*, Chicago

Das Gupta, J. (1970) *Language, Conflict and National Development: Group Politics and National Policy in India*, Berkeley

Davis, S.R. (1978) *The Federal Principle: A Journey Through Time in Quest of a Meaning*, Berkeley

Deuerlein, E. (1972) *Föderalismus: Die historischen und philosophischen Grundlagen des föderativen Prinzips*, Bonn

Deutsch, K. (1953) *Nationalism and Social Communication: An Inquiry into the Foundations of Nationality*, Cambridge, Mass.

Diamond, M. (1959) 'Democracy and *The Federalist*: A Reconsideration of the Framers' Intent', *American Political Science Review*, 53, 1, pp. 52-68

Dicey, A.V. (1885, 1915) *The Law of the Constitution*, London

Dikshit, R.D. (1971) 'Military Interpretation of Federal Constitutions: A Critique', *Journal of Politics*, 33, 1, pp. 180-9

Duchacek, I.D. (1970) *Comparative Federalism: The Territorial Dimension of Politics*, New York

Durkheim, E. (1893) *De la Division du travail social: étude sur l'organisation des sociétés supérieures*, Paris

—— (1897) *Le Suicide: étude de sociologie*, Paris

Duverger, M. (1959) *Political Parties: Their Organization and Activity in the Modern State*, London

Earle, V. (ed.) (1968) *Federalism: Infinite Variety in Theory and Practice*, Itasca, Ill.

. Eckstein, H. (1966) *Division and Cohesion in Democracy: A Study of Norway*, Princeton

Elazar, D.J. (1962) *The American Partnership*, Chicago

Elbow, M.H. (1953) *French Corporative Theory, 1789-1948*, New York

Embree, E.T. (1973) 'Pluralism and National Integration: The Indian Experience', *Journal of International Affairs*, 27, 1, pp. 41-52

Etzioni, A. (1965) *Political Unification: A Comparative Study of Leaders and Forces*, New York

Favareille, R. (1919) *Réforme administrative par l'autonomie et la responsabilité des fonctions*, Paris

Figgis, J.N. (1907, 1931) *Studies of Political Thought from Gerson to Grotius, 1414-1625*, Cambridge

Finer, H. (1949) *The Theory and Practice of Modern Government*, New York

Follett, M.P. (1918) *The New State*, New York

Franck, T.M. (ed.) (1968) *Why Federations Fail: An Inquiry into the Requisites for Successful Federalism*, New York

Freeman, E.A. (1863) *History of Federal Government: From the Foundation of the Achaian League to the Disruption of the United States*, London

Friedrich, C.J. (1968) *Trends of Federalism in Theory and Practice*, London

――― (1974) *Limited Government: A Comparison*, Englewood Cliffs, NJ

Golay, J.F. (1958) *The Founding of the Federal Republic of Germany*, Chicago

Gough, J. (1957) (2nd edn) *The Social Contract: A Critical Study of its Development*, Oxford

Greaves, H.R.G. (1940) *Federal Union in Practice*, London

Greenstone, J.D. (1975) 'Group Theories', in F.I. Greenstein and N.W. Polsby (eds) *Handbook of Political Science*, Vol. 2, pp. 243-318

Grotius, H. (1625, 1646: Amsterdam) *De Iure Belli ac Pacis*, Paris

Guyau, J.M. (1885) *Esquisse d'une morale sans obligation ni sanction*, Paris

Hamerow, T.S. (1958) *Restoration, Revolution, Reaction: Economics and Politics in Germany, 1815-1871*, Princeton, NJ

Hamilton, A., Jay, J. and Madison, J. (pseud. 'Publius') (1788) *The Federalist: (A Collection of Essays, Written in Favour of the New Constitution as Agreed upon by the Federal Convention, Sept. 17, 1787)*, 2 vols, New York

Harrison, R.J. (1980) *Pluralism and Corporatism: The Political Evolution of Modern Democracies*, London

Hazlewood, A. (1967) *African Integration and Disintegration: Case Studies in Economic and Political Union*, London

Hennessy, C.A.M. (1962) *The Federal Republic in Spain: Pí y Margall and the Federal Republican Movement, 1868-74*, Oxford

Hennessy, J. and Charles-Brun, J. (1940) *Le Principe fédératif*, Paris

Hennessy, J. (1942) *Diplomatie nouvelle et fédéralisme*, Paris

Hicks, U.K. *et al.* (1961) *Federalism and Economic Growth in Underdeveloped Countries*, London

Hicks, U. (1978) *Federalism: Failure and Success*, London

Himmelfarb, G. (1952) *Lord Acton: A Study in Conscience and Politics*, Chicago

Hobbes, T. (1651) *Leviathan*, London

Holmes, J. and Sharman, C. (1977) *The Australian Federal System*, Sydney

Hughes, E.C. (1963) *French Canada in Transition*, Chicago

Hutchins, R.M. (1961) *Two Faces of Federalism: An Outline of an Argument about Pluralism, Unity and Law*, Santa Barbara, Calif.

Jackson, R.H. (1941) *The Struggle for Judicial Supremacy: A Study of Crisis in American Power Politics*, New York

Jacob, P.E. and Toscano, J.V. (eds) (1964) *The Integration of Political Communities*, Philadelphia

Kelsen, H. (1948, 1961: 2nd edn) *General Theory of Law and the State*, trans. A. Wedberg, New York

King, P. (1967) *Fear of Power: An Analysis of Anti-Statism in Three French Writers*, London

—— (1968) 'An Ideological Fallacy', in P. King and B. Parekh (eds), *Politics and Experience: Essays Presented to Professor Michael Oakeshott on the Occasion of his Retirement*, pp. 341–94, Cambridge

—— (1974) *The Ideology of Order: A Comparative Analysis of Jean Bodin and Thomas Hobbes*, London

—— (1977) 'Ideology as Politics', *The Political Quarterly*, 48, 1, pp. 78–83

Kohn, H. (1956) *Nationalism and Liberty: The Swiss Example*, London

Kornhauser, W. (1960) *The Politics of Mass Society*, London

Kropotkin, P. (1885) *Paroles d'un Révolté*, Paris

—— (1886) *Law and Authority: An Anarchist Essay*, London

—— (1892) *Anarchist Morality*, London

—— (1892a) (2nd edn) *L'Anarchie dans la révolution socialiste*, Paris

—— (1896) *L'Anarchie: sa philosophie, son idéal*, Paris

—— (1898) *Fields, Factories and Workshops*, London

—— (1902) *Mutual Aid: A Factor of Evolution*, London

Languet, H. (pseud. S.J. Brutus) (1579, 1581) *Vindiciae contra tyrannos: sive de Principis in populum populique in principem legitima potestate*, Basle

Larsen, J.A.O. (1968) *Greek Federal States*, Oxford

Laski, H.J. (1939) 'The Obsolescence of Federalism', *New Republic*, 98, 1274, pp. 367–9

Lee Kuan Yew (1961) *The Battle for Merger*, Singapore

Le Fur, L.E. (1896) *L'État fédéral et la confédération d'états*, Paris

Lewis, W.A. (1965) *Politics in West Africa*, London

Lipset, S.M. (1960) *Political Man: The Social Bases of Politics*, New York

Livingston, W.S. (1956) *Federalism and Constitutional Change*, Oxford

—— (1963) *Federalism in the Commonwealth: A Bibliographical Commentary*, London

Locke, J. (1690) *Two Treatises of Government*, London

MacMahon, A. (ed.) (1955) *Federalism: Mature and Emergent*, Garden City

Mallory, J.R. (1941) 'Compact Theory of Confederation', *Dalhousie Review*, 21 (Oct), pp. 342–51

—— (1954) *Social Credit and The Federal Power in Canada*, Toronto

—— (1974) 'Le Système constitutionnel canadien', in *Corpus Constitutionnel du Canada*, Vol. 2 (1), pp. 101–63

Marc, A. (1961) *Dialectique du déchaînement, fondements philosophique du fédéralisme*, Paris

Mariana, J. de (1599) *De rege et regis institutione*, Libri III, Toleti

McKinnon, V.S. (1964) *Comparative Federalism: A Study in Judicial Interpretation*, Hague

McWhinney, E.W. (1962) *Constitutionalism in Germany and the Federal Constitu-*

tional Court, Leyden

―――― (1965) (2nd edn) *Comparative Federalism: States' Rights and National Power*, Toronto

―――― (1966) *Federal Constitution-Making for a Multi-National World*, Leyden

Means, G.P. (1970) *Malaysian Politics*, New York

Meekison, J.P. (ed.) (1968, 1971) *Canadian Federalism: Myth or Reality*, Toronto

Menon, V.P. (1956) *The Integration of the Indian States*, New York

Merkl, P. (1963) *The Origin of the West German Republic*, London

Mill, J.S. (1861) *Considerations on Representative Government*, London

Mogi, S. (1931) *The Problem of Federalism: A Study in the History of Political Theory*, 2 vols, London

Morin, J.-Y. (1963) *Le Fédéralisme: théorie et critique*, Montréal

Morley, F. (1959) *Freedom and Federalism*, Chicago

Murray, J.O. (1973) *Government and People*, London

Nawiasky, H. (1920) *Der Bundesstaat als Rechtsbegriff*, Tübingen

Olivier-Martin, F. (1938) *L'Organisation corporative de la France d'ancien régime*, Paris

Paul-Boncour, J. (1900) *Le Fédéralisme économique*, Paris

―――― (1905) (with C.M.P. Maurras) *Un Débat nouveau sur la République et la décentralisation*, Toulouse

Pennock, J.R. (1959) 'Federal and Unitary Government – Disharmony and Frustration', *Behavioral Science*, 4, pp. 147–57

Pflanze, O. (1963) *Bismarck and the Development of Germany: The Period of Unification, 1815–1871*, Princeton, NJ

Pierson, W.W. and Gil, F.G. (1957) *Governments of Latin America*, New York

Pí y Margall, F. (1854) *La Reacción y la Revolución*, Madrid

―――― (1880) *La Federación*, Barcelona

―――― (1931) *Lecciones de Federalismo*, Recopiladas por J. Pí y Arsuaga, Barcelona

Proudhon, P.-J. (1863) *Du Principe fédératif et de la nécessité de reconstituer le parti de la révolution*, Paris

Provencher, J. (1977) *René Levesque: Portrait of a Québécois*, Markham, Ont.

Pufendorf, S. von (1672) *De Iure Naturae et Gentium*, Libri VIII, London

Pyziur, E. (1955) *The Doctrine of Anarchism of Michael A. Bakunin*, Milwaukee, Wisc.

Ratnam, K.J. (1961) 'Constitutional Government and the "Plural Society": Some General Observations', *Journal of Southeast Asian History*, 2, 3, pp. 1–10

Rau, B.N. (1960) *India's Constitution in the Making*, Bombay

Read, C. (ed.) (1938) *The Constitution Reconsidered*, New York

Renouvier, C. (1869) *Science de la morale*, Paris

Riha, T. (ed.) (1964) *Readings in Russian Civilization*, 3 vols, Chicago

Riker, W.H. (1964) *Federalism: Origin, Operation, Significance*, Boston

―――― (1969) 'Six Books in Search of A Subject or Does Federalism Exist and Does It Matter?', *Comparative Politics*, 2, pp. 135–46

―――― (1975) 'Federalism', in F.I. Greenstein and N.W. Polsby (eds) *Handbook of Political Science*, 5, pp. 93–172

Rioux, M. and Martin, Y. (eds) (1964) *French-Canadian Society*, Toronto

Rockefeller, N.A. (1962) *The Future of Federalism*, Cambridge, Mass.

Rokkan, S. (1966) 'Norway: Numerical Democracy and Corporate Pluralism', in

R.A. Dahl (ed.) *Political Oppositions in Western Democracies*, New Haven and London, pp. 70–115

Rousseau, J.-J. (1762) *Du Contrat social*, Amsterdam

Saint-Simon, C.H. (1814) *De la Réorganisation de la société européenne, ou de la Nécessité et des Moyens de rassembler les peuples de l'Europe en un seul corps politique, en conservant à chacun son indépendence nationale*, Paris

Sartori, G. (1976) *Parties and Party System: A Framework for Analysis*, vol. 1, Cambridge

Sawer, G. (1976) (2nd edn) *Modern Federalism*, Carlton, Vic.

Schiller, A.A. (1955) *The Formation of Federal Indonesia*, Hague

Schlesinger, R. (1945) *Federalism in Eastern and Central Europe*, London

Schmitter, P.C. (1971) *Interest Conflict and Political Change in Brazil*, Stanford

Schwan, A. (1969) 'Plurale Gesellschaft und Katholische Kirche', *Liberal*, 11 (3 Mar.), pp. 181–97

Seliger, M. (1976) *Ideology and Politics*, London

Serbyn, R. *et al.* (1971) *Fédéralisme et Nations*, Montréal

Sharma, B.M. (1951) *Federalism in Theory and Practice*, 2 vols, Chandausi, India

Sheridan, L.A. *et al.* (1961) *Malaya and Singapore, The Borneo Territories: The Development of Their Laws and Constitutions*, London

Shoup, P. (1968) *Communism and the Yugoslav National Question*, New York

Sidgwick, H. (1891, 1919) *The Elements of Politics*, London

Sidjanski, D. (1956) *Fédéralisme amphictyonique: éléments de système et tendance internationale*, Lausanne

Silva, R. (1944) *Au Service de la Paix: l'idée fédéraliste*, Neuchatel

Simandjuntak, B. (1969) *Malayan Federalism 1945–1963*, Kuala Lumpur

Simmel, G. (1922) *Soziologie*, München

Solomon, D. (1978) *Australia's Government and Politics*, Melbourne

Spencer, H. (1884) *The Man versus the State*, London

Suarez, F. (1612) *Tractatus de legibus ac Deo legislatore*, Conimbricae

Tarlton, C.D. (1965) 'Symmetry and Asymmetry as Elements of Federalism: A Theoretical Speculation', *The Journal of Politics*, 27, pp. 861–74

——— (1967) 'Federalism, Political Energy, and Entropy: Implications of an Analogy', *Western Political Quarterly*, 3–4, pp. 866–74

Taylor, A.J.P. (1964) *The Origins of the Second World War*, Harmondsworth

Thomson, D.C. (ed.) (1973) *Quebec Society and Politics: Views from the Inside*, Toronto

Tocqueville, A.C. de (1835–40) *De la Démocratie en Amérique*, 2 vols, Paris

Trudeau, P.-E. (1968) *Federalism and the French Canadians*, Toronto

Vallières, P. (1971) *White Niggers of America: The Precocious Autobiography of a Quebec 'Terrorist'*, trans. J. Pinkham, New York

Vile, M.J.C. (1961) *The Structure of American Federalism*, London

——— (1967) *Constitutionalism and the Separation of Powers*, Oxford

Voyenne, B. (1976) *Histoire de l'idée fédéraliste: les sources*, Paris

Watts, R.L. (1966) *New Federations: Experiments in the Commonwealth*, Oxford

Wheare, K.C. (1946, 1953) *Federal Government*, London

——— (1951) *Modern Constitutions*, London

——— (1963) *Legislatures*, Oxford

Wildavsky, A. (ed.) (1967) *American Federalism in Perspective*, Boston

Wilson, W. (1956) *Congressional Government*, New York

Woodcock, G. and Avakumović, I. (1950) *The Anarchist Prince: A Biographical Study of Peter Kropotkin*, London and New York

INDEX

Absolutism 21-3, 92-3, 137
Achaean League 133
Acton 42, 62, 63
Africa 30, 66, 71, 81, 85, 90, 108, 109, 124
Albertini, M. 32
Althusius, J. 57
Amellier, M. 94
America *see* USA
Analytical Political Theory 10
Anarchism 23, 29; and decentralism 39-55; definition 23, 67; *The Federalist* on 29
Arab League 145
Argentina 71
Aron, R. 21, 32, 34
Asia 71
Australia 32, 58, 71, 73, 77, 81, 86, 88, 94, 109, 121, 146, 147
Austria 98
Avakumović, I. 43

Bakunin, M. 23, 29, 31, 41-3
Balance (of powers) 56-68, 128
Bangladesh 81, 109, 119
Belgium 124
Bermuda 123
Bernard, A. 56
Bernaus, A.J. 40
Berneri, C. 43
Bernier, I. 113
Bicameralism 94-5
Birch, A.H. 35, 80, 84
Bodin, J. 22, 26, 29, 133
Bonn constitution 44, 57, 97, 98
Booth, J.W. 135
Borel, E. 113, 114, 115
Brandt, W. 98
Brazil 23, 71, 109, 147
Britain *see* United Kingdom
British Empire 139, 145
British North America (BNA) Act 105
Brugmans, H. 21, 32, 34, 35, 38, 56, 82, 100
Bryce, J. 43

Calhoun, J. 43, 44, 62, 108, 110, 114, 134
California 91
Camargo, P.P. 38
Cambodia 147
Cameroon 94
Canada 32, 34, 58, 71, 73, 81, 86, 88, 94, 95, 104-5, 109, 111, 121, 147
Centralism, centralist federalism 21-38, 121, 125
Centralization, degrees of; incommensurable types of 128-9, 136-7; Kelsen on 122-3; Livingston on 126-8; Riker on 124-5
China 123, 147
Clay, L. 98, 99
Confederation, examples of 133; u/c/f typology 133-42
Constitutionalism 23, 67-8, 88, 89, 91, 144-5; and Dicey 143; and polyarchy 121-2, 141-2, 147-8
Contract, theory 56-8, 78-9, 84-5; and secession 108-13; and separation of powers 91-2; enforcement 103-4; federation as continuing 102-7; federation as original 96-101; Hobbes on 57, 78-9; Rousseau 57; terms of 102-3
Cook, R. 108
Co-ordinate powers 59, 113-20
Corbo, C. 30, 41
Curtis, L. 21, 32, 35

Davis, S.R. 22, 37, 61, 71, 80, 94, 96, 114, 126, 137, 139
Decentralism, decentralist federalism 39-55; and anarchism 44-55; and Bakunin 41-3; and Calhoun 44; and Guyau 46; and Kropotkin 43, 46, 51-3; and Pí y Margall 39-40; and Proudhon 40-1; and *Reichskonkordat* case 54-5
Democracy, definition 89, 92, 141; and federation 88-95
Deuerlein, E. 21
Dicey, A.V. 114, 134, 143, 145
Dikshit, R.D. 98
Duchacek, I. 71, 114, 115, 129, 143

156

Dulles, J.F. 98

Egypt 123, 133
England *see* United Kingdom
Eritrea 147
Ethiopia 147
Europe 30-5, 39-43, 71, 74-5, 81, 82, 133, 146-7

Federalism, and pluralism 19-23; and federation 74-6; as balance 56-68; as centralist 24-38; as decentralist 39-55; as pluralist ideology 19-21
Federalist, The 24-30, 36, 44, 114, 134
Federation, and federalism 20-2, 74-6; and bicameralism 94-5; and coordinate powers 113-20; and constitutionalism 145, 146-8; and equality of representation 89-91; and secession 108-20; and separation of powers 91-3; and sovereignty 141-2; and typology (u/c/f) 133-9; and unification 147; as a degree of centralization 121-9; as continuing contract 102-7; as non-absolutist 88-9; as original contract 96-102; as response to threat 79-85; criteria 142-3; definition 139-41; empirical investigation 76-87; entrenchment 142; examples of 71; Method of definition 71-3, 144-5
Fichte, J. 57
Figgis, J.N. 43, 64, 99
Follett, M.P. 74
Fourier, C. 30, 43
France 30, 32, 34, 37, 68, 82, 93, 98, 99, 105, 111-12, 123, 124, 133
Franck, T.M. 85-6
Freeman, E. 43, 56
Friedrich, C.J. 38, 56, 86

Gambia 147
Gandhi, M. 53
Gaulle, C. de 111
Germany 32, 34, 35-6, 37, 39, 82, 84, 89, 97, 98, 99, 100-1, 108
Ghana 77
Gierke, O. von 43
Godwin, W. 30
Golay, J.F. 99
Gold Coast 139
Gough, J. 57

Greece 133
Grotius, H. 29, 57
Guggisberg, G. 139
Guyau, J.M. 46, 51

Halévy, D. 32
Hamerow, T.S. 98
Hamilton, A. 24, 114, 134
Hennessy, J. 31-2, 35, 37, 39
Herrarte, A. 24, 38
Hicks, U.K. 88, 89, 143
Himmelfarb, G. 62
Hitler, A. 39
Hobbes, T. 22, 25, 26, 27, 29, 30, 31, 34, 36, 57, 62, 79, 84, 85, 92, 115, 133
Hutchins, R.M. 21

Ideology, definition 19-20; and centralist federalism 24-38; and decentralist federalism 39-55; and federalist balance 56-68; and federation 74-6; varieties of federalist 19-23; varieties of pluralist 19
India 71, 88, 89, 104, 105, 109, 126, 145, 146
Indonesia 77, 147
Inge, D. 65
Iran 129
Ireland 34
Italy 34, 55, 121

Jackson, R.H. 21
Jamaica 90, 119
Japan 100
Jay, J. 24

Kant, I. 57, 67
Kelsen, H. 121-4, 125, 126, 138
Kenya 121, 133
King, M.L. 53
Krabbe, H. 43
Kropotkin, P. 23, 29, 43, 45-6, 51-3

Languet, H. 57
Laos 147
Laski, H.J. 43, 114
Lebanon 121, 147
Le Fur, L.E. 113, 114, 115
Lenin, V.I. 43, 110
Levesque, R. 108, 111
Lewis, W.A. 90
Liberalism 42, 43

Liechtenstein 123
Lincoln, A. 135
Livingston, W.S. 90, 114, 126-9
Livingstone, D. 66
Locke, J. 34, 57, 58

Machiavelli, N. 37
McWhinney, E.W. 38, 55, 100
Madison, J. 24
Malaysia 71, 77, 80, 85, 119
Mallory, J.R. 108
Marc, A. 20, 56, 74
Mariana, J. de 57
Mauritius 90
Marx, K. 63
Massachusetts 36
Meekison, J.P. 90, 114, 126, 128
Mexico 71
Mill, J.S. 114
Mogi, S. 43
Montesquieu 62
Morocco 147
Moscow 43

Nawiasky, H. 113
Netherlands 143
New England Confederacy 133
New Zealand 32, 77
Niedersachsen 54
Nigeria 35, 37, 71, 77, 80, 90, 97,
    119
Nkrumah, K. 90
North Atlantic Treaty Organization
    133
Northern Ireland 34, 143
North German Confederation 133
North Korea 147
Norway 68

Oceana 71
Organization of African Unity 133
Ottoman Empire 123
Owen, R. 30

Pakistan 81, 94, 119
Paolini, E. 32
Park, M. 66
Pétain, M. 31-2
Pflanze, O. 98
Pí y Margall, F. 39-40, 41, 43
Pluralism 19-24, 74-5
Poland 77, 129
Portugal 123
Powers, separation of 91-3; *see also*

Balance
Proudhon, P.J. 20, 31, 39-41, 42, 43,
    56, 57, 74, 96
Provencher, J. 108
'Publius' 24
Pufendorf, S. 29, 57
Pyziur, E. 42

Quebec 34, 81, 111-12, 117, 121

Rawls, J. 57
Reagan, R. 9, 13
Reichskonkordat case 54-5
Renouvier, C. 57
Representation, Equality of 89-91
Rhode Island 91
Rights, individual and group 58-9
Riha, T. 110
Riker, W.H. 33-6, 37, 79, 82-6, 98,
    100, 114, 124-5, 126
Rousseau, J-J. 57, 92
Rules, divergence of 47-8

Sahara 147
Saint-Simon, C.H. 30-1, 35, 37, 41,
    43
Sawer, G. 71, 97
Schmid, C. 99
Scotland 123, 143
Secession, and contract 108-13; and
    coordinate powers 113-20
Seliger, M. 20, 76
Senegal 147
Serbyn, R. 30, 41, 56
Sidjanski, D. 108, 124, 145
Silva, R. 32
Singapore 119
South Africa 32, 81
South America 71
South Korea 147
Sovereignty: and contract 108-13;
    and coordinate powers 113-20;
    and democratic absolutism 92-3;
    and federation 133-45; and
    finality of decision 115; and
    secession 108-20; as unilateral
    treaty interpretation 108; classical
    doctrine 25, 114-15, 133-4,
    137-8, 141; definition of 141;
    Federalist view of 22-30; *qua*
    degree of centralization (in federa-
    tion) 135-6
Spence, W. 30
Spencer, H. 57

Spinoza, B. de 29, 133
Stalin, J. 110
Stanley, H. 66
Suarez, F. 57
Sudan 71, 81
Sweden 68, 93, 94, 111
Switzerland 31, 37, 58, 71, 79, 88,
    94, 97, 104, 105, 109, 121, 133,
    146
Syria 147

Taiwan 147
Tanganyika 89
Tanzania 61, 71, 81
Threat, as required for federal union
    33-7, 79-86
Timor 147
Tocqueville, A.C. de 42, 43, 114
Trotsky, L. 110

U/C/F typology 133-9; rationale of
    134-5
Unitary States, in u/c/f typology
    122, 124-5, 133-42; redundancy
    of 138-9, 142
United Arab Emirates 88
United Kingdom 30, 32, 37, 39, 81,
    82, 99, 103, 104, 105, 121, 123,
    133, 143
United States of America 22-3,
    24-30, 32, 34, 35, 36, 37, 39, 44,
    53, 55, 58, 59, 60, 61, 71, 73, 77,
    79, 81, 82, 84, 86, 88, 89, 91, 94,
    95, 97, 98, 99, 100, 105, 109,
    119, 121, 124, 133, 134, 139,
    145, 146, 147
USSR 71, 82, 98, 108-12, 117, 120,
    121

Venezuela 71
Vietnam 147
Voyenne, B. 20, 44, 56, 80, 96

Wales 43
Watts, R.L. 56, 64, 113, 127-8
West Germany 35, 54, 59, 71, 81, 84,
    101, 121
West Indies 81, 85, 90
West Irian 147
Wheare, K.C. 59, 114, 134, 138, 145
Woodcock, G. 43

Yugoslavia 71, 77, 94, 97, 105

Zanzibar 89